MW00827285

Archaic Latin Verse

Archaic Latin Verse

Mario Erasmo
UNIVERSITY OF GEORGIA

Focus Classical Library

 *an imprint of*
Hackett Publishing Company, Inc.
Indianapolis/Cambridge

Archaic Latin Verse

Copyright © 2004 Mario Erasmo

Previously published by Focus Publishing/R. Pullins Company

Focus an imprint of
  Hackett Publishing Company
P.O. Box 44937
Indianapolis, Indiana 46244-0937

www.hackettpublishing.com

All rights are reserved.

Printed in the United States of America

19 18 17 16 15   3 4 5 6 7

ISBN 13: 978-1-58510-043-9

Preface

The earliest Roman poems survive only in fragmentary form. What fragments that do survive are often overlooked in the classroom due to the difficulty of incorporating them into survey courses of Latin literature or courses devoted to epic poetry. In large part this is due to the absence of an available edition that focuses exclusively on this material. W.W. Merry's *Selected Fragments of Roman Poetry* (Oxford, 1898), which includes only a sampling of the early fragments, is now out of print and somewhat outdated for college classroom use. E. Diehl's *Poetarum Romanorum Veterum Reliquiae* (Berlin, 1911, reprinted 1967), A. Ernout's *Recueil de Textes Latines Archaïques* (Paris, 1957), which includes both prose and verse selections, and W. Morel's *Fragmenta Poetarum Latinorum* (Stuttgart, 1927², reprinted 1963), do not include a commentary. Monographs on individual poets also offer challenges for classroom use: commentaries devoted to Naevius' *Bellum Punicum* are in Latin (W. Strzelecki, *Cn. Naevii Belli Punici Carminis quae supersunt,* Lipsiae, 1964), or Italian (Marino Barchiesi, *Nevio epico*, Padova, 1962; Scevola Mariotti, *Il Bellum Punicum e l'arte di Nevio,* Roma, 1955; and Enzo V. Marmorale, *Naevius Poeta*, Firenze, 1953). Ennius has fared better in English with excellent commentaries on the *Annales* (Otto Skutsch, *The Annals of Q. Ennius*, Oxford, 1985), the tragedies (H.D. Jocelyn, *The Tragedies of Ennius*, Cambridge, 1967), and other poems (E. Courtney, *Fragmentary Latin Poets*, Oxford, 1993); but these are too detailed (and costly) to assign for survey courses, where only a few class sessions might be devoted to archaic poets. Other tragic and comic texts are found in non-English editions or in English but with no commentary: L. Mueller, *Livi Andronici et Cn. Naevi Fabularum Reliquiae* (Berlin, 1885); Otto Ribbeck, *Scaenicae Romanorum Poesis Fragmenta: Vol. 1 Tragicorum Romanorum Fragmenta* (*TRF*) (Lipsiae, 1897³); with commentary in his *Römische Tragödie* (Leipzig, 1875) and comic fragments in his *Scaenicae Romanorum Poesis Fragmenta: Vol. 2 Comicorum Romanorum Fragmenta* (Lipsiae, 1898); M. Valsa, *Marcus Pacuvius Poète Tragique* (Paris, 1957); I. D'Anna, ed., *M. Pacuvii Fragmenta* (Roma, 1967); P. Magno, *Marco Pacuvio, i frammenti con intro., trad., comm.* (Milano, 1967); Q. Franchella,

Lucii Accii tragoediaraum fragmenta (Bologna, 1968); V. D'Anto, *I frammenti delle tragedie di L. Acio* (Lecce, 1980); J. Dangel, *Accius Oeuvres (fragments)* (Paris, 1995); and E.H. Warmington's Loeb editions: *Remains of Old Latin*, Volumes 1-4 for the texts and translations of all archaic authors. For Lucilius' fragments, F. Marx's *C. Lucilii Carminum Reliquiae* (Amsterdam, 1904), contains a commentary in Latin.

The aim of this text is to make select fragments of archaic Latin verse available to students by providing the most accessible selections arranged by genre, rather than author, with brief explanatory and grammatical notes necessary for a first translation. I highlight the influence of the *carmen* on subsequent Latin poetry; Livius Andronicus, Naevius, and Ennius on Vergil's *Aeneid* and Horace's *Odes*; the dramatists on Seneca; Caecilius on the development of Roman comedy; and Lucilius on the satires of Horace and Juvenal. I follow the chronological order of literary developments within genres which has inevitably led to a sequential listing of some works when a synchronistic development across genres is more accurate. Since the plays of Plautus and Terence are available in detailed commentaries, they are not included here. I do not provide an *apparatus criticus* or cite the ancient sources for the fragments since these are provided by the cited editions.

This reprinting contains corrections and a few minor additions to the commentary. My aim remains to provide a text that allows teachers maximum flexibility in providing their own interpretation to students when incorporating these fragments into their translation courses. Students should consult texts listed in the bibliography for more detailed commentaries.

June, 2004

Table of Contents

Editions of Fragments

Barchiesi, Marino. 1962. *Nevio epico*. Padova.

Barrile, Resta, ed. and trad. 1969. *Accius, Lucius: Frammenti dalle tragedie e dalle preteste*. Bologna.

Cichorius. C. 1922. *Die Fragmente historischen Inhalts aus Naevius Bellum Punicum: Römische Studien*. Leipzig.

Courtney, Edward. 1993. *Fragmentary Latin Poets*. Oxford.

Dangel, Jacqueline. 1995. *Accius: Oeuvres*. Paris.

D'Anna, Ioannes, ed. 1967. *M. Pacuvii Fragmenta*. Roma.

D'Antò, Vicenzo. 1980. *I frammenti delle tragedie di L. Accio*. Lecce.

Diehl, Ernst. 1967, reprint of 1911. *Poetarum Romanorum Veterum Reliquiae*. Berlin.

Ernout, A. 1957. *Recueil de Textes Latines Archaïques*. Paris.

Franchella, Quirinus. 1968. *Lucii Acii tragoediarum fragmenta*. Bologna.

Jocelyn, H.D. 1967. *The Tragedies of Ennius*. Cambridge.

Klotz, Alfred. 1953. *Scaenicorum Romanorum fragmenta*. Munich.

Magno, Pietro. 1977. *Marco Pacuvio, i frammenti con intro., trad.,comm.* Milano.

Mariotti, Scevola. 1955. *Il Bellum Punicum e l'arte di Nevio*. Roma.

Marmorale, Enzo V. 1953. *Naevius Poeta*. Firenze.

Marx, F. 1963, reprint of 1904. *C. Lucilii Carminum Reliquiae*. Amsterdam.

Morel, Willy. 1963, reprint of 1927[2]. *Fragmenta Poetarum Latinorum Epicorum et Lyricorum. Praeter Ennium et Lucilium.* Stuttgart.

Mueller, Lucianus. 1854. *Q. Enni Carminum Reliquiae.* Petropolis.

Mueller, Lucianus. 1885. *Livi Andronici et Cn. Naevi Fabularum Reliquiae.* Berlin.

Ribbeck, Otto. 1897[3]. *Scaenicae Romanorum Poesis Fragmenta, Vol. 1: Tragicorum Romanorum Fragmenta, (TRF).* Lipsiae.

Ribbeck, Otto. 1898. *Scaenicae Romanorum Poesis Fragmenta, Vol. 2: Comicorum Romanorum Fragmenta, (CRF).* Lipsiae.

Ribbeck, Otto. 1875. *Römische Tragödie (RT).* Leipzig.

Skutsch, Otto. 1985. *The Annals of Q. Ennius.* Oxford.

Strzelecki, W. 1964. *Cn. Naevii Belli Punici Carminis quae supersunt.* Lipsiae.

Vahlen, Iohannes. 1854, reprinted 1903 and 1928. *Ennianae Poesis Reliquiae.* Lipsiae. (The 1928 edition reproduced 1963, Amsterdam.)

Valsa, M. 1957. *Marcus Pacuvius Poète Tragique.* Paris.

Warmington, E.H. 1935, reprinted1988. *Remains of Old Latin, Volume 1: Ennius and Caecilius (ROL I).* Loeb Classical Library. Cambridge, MA and London.

Warmington, E.H. 1936, reprinted 1982. *Remains of Old Latin, Volume 2: Livius Andronicus, Naevius, Pacuvius and Accius (ROL II).* Loeb Classical Library. Cambridge, MA and London.

Warmington, E.H. 1940, reprinted 1979. *Remains of Old Latin, Volume 4: Archaic Inscriptions (ROL IV).* Loeb Classical Library. Cambridge, MA and London.

Introduction

Latin literature begins in 240 BCE when Livius Andronicus presented his first tragedy (and comedy?) in the victory celebrations following the end of the First Punic War (264-241). This is the earliest date that survives even though Livius' *Odyssia* may actually pre-date this first play. Before either of Livius' works, Latin "literature" in Italy was oral. How did Italians resist written literature for so long in light of the wide-ranging literary achievements of the Greeks? To answer this question, in part, one must consider the nature of oral poetry that existed prior to 240 BCE, and explain how a native Italian phenomenon with Greek influence became the basis of Roman poetry and literature. One cannot turn to Greek experience for an answer since Greeks endured the upheavals of wars, political turmoil, and colonization for centuries and produced poetry as a response to and an escape from these experiences. Whatever the answer, and certainty is impossible, once begun, Roman literature was bold and brilliant and blossomed quickly into various literary genres. Yet, despite Greek influence, it was never far removed from its oral and native Italian roots, witnessed by the extensive and long lasting influence of the native *carmen*-style verse techniques. The versatility of early Latin poets is demonstrated by the wide range of genres that were undertaken almost simultaneously.

Latin poetry arises out of a native oral tradition centered upon the *carmen,* which originally signified a formulaic utterance, whether in verse (in *versus quadratus*) or in prose. Examples survive in the form of prayers, charms, curses, laws (the Twelve Tables), and rhymes.[1] Funeral orations and dinner songs, which would fill out this list, do not survive.[2] The *carmen*

---

1 Cicero laments that school children no longer memorize/recite the Twelve Tables: *discebamus pueri XII (tabulas) ut carmen necessarium, quas iam nemo discit* (*de Legibus* 2.59).

2 These dinner songs were lost by Cicero's day: *Brutus* 75: *atque utinam exstarent illa carmina, quae multis saeculis ante suam aetatem in epulis esse cantitata a singulis convivis de clarorum virorum laudibus in Originibus scriptum reliquit Cato; Tusculans* 4.3: *gravissimus auctor in Originibus dixit Cato*

10

influenced the development of the Saturnian verse, a native Italian meter (Caesius Bassus claims it came from Greece, but its origins are obscure) that emphasizes rhythm (word accent) rather than quantity and achieves its highest artistic expression under Livius Andronicus and Naevius. Solemn in sound and heavy in alliteration, the *carmen* and Saturnian would exercise a far-reaching and wide-ranging influence on subsequent poetic developments.

The legal, religious, proverbial, and funereal context of oral poetry may account for the long duration of archaic forms in written poetry, from the early poets even to the Augustan poets (and beyond), who incorporated an archaic vocabulary and *carmen*-style verse techniques in their works.[3] Archaic words could add dignity to a description and confer the approbation of tradition but they could also call attention to their former contexts by their appearance in new contemporary contexts. Horace, for example, styled himself a *vates* and called his Odes *Carmina*, thereby transforming the archaic *carmen* into a highly polished poem. Unless one is aware of the archaic verse tradition behind these terms, the originality and impact of Horace's claims are lost.

Before this archaizing tendency was applied to poetry, it was a feature of epigraphic texts. The anonymous authors of these inscriptions peppered their epitaphs with archaic language more appropriate to an earlier age and yet this language was consciously at odds with the poetic style of the epitaph. We find modern spellings and contemporary concepts together with archaic forms but we also find archaisms in epitaphs whose poetic style betrays a later date when the language does not. In addition to the continual use of archaizing forms, we find the Saturnian meter used in epitaphs until at least the mid-first century BCE, long after its disappearance as a literary meter.

Livius Andronicus was brought to Rome (probably in boyhood) as a prisoner of war from the surrender of Tarentum in 272 BCE, and was given the name of his owner Livius Salinator. It is significant for his later Latin adaptations (not translations) of Greek poetry and drama that he was a native Greek speaker who was familiar with the meters from epic, tragedy, and comedy. We cannot assume, therefore, that he could not write Latin verse in hexameter when he composed his *Odyssia* in Saturnians. Perhaps his

---

morem apud maiores hunc epularum fuisse, ut deinceps qui accubarent canerent ad tibiam clarorum virorum laudes atque virtutes (cf. *Tusculans* 1.3). Varro (*de vita populi Romani*, Book 2, quoted at Nonius 77.2), claims that youths sang, rather than reclining old men as in Cicero's version: *in conviviis pueri modesti ut cantarent carmina antiqua in quibus laudes erant maiorum et assa voce et cum tibicine.*

3 This archaizing tendency is not limited to literature. In the *Brutus* (210-211), Cicero illustrates the importance of spoken language on oratorical skill through the example of the female descendants of Scipio Africanus who preserve his purity of diction (*Latine loqui*), thus suggesting an archaic speech pattern among certain aristocratic women.

preference for the native Italian Saturnian, rather than the Greek hexameter, reveals that he was striving for an ancient Italian equivalent to approximate the antiquity and solemnity of Homer's verse. Livius' use of language, already archaic by his day, points in this direction. His choice of the *Odyssey* rather than the *Iliad* for translation may be due to the fact that it was used as a classroom text — perhaps as a teacher he felt that his young students would enjoy the fantasy world of the *Odyssey* more than the death and mortality focus of the *Iliad*.

As with epic, Livius' contributions to Roman drama were enormous.[4] Livius' innovations were adopted by subsequent dramatists, which explains the particular features of Roman drama that distinguishes it from Greek drama. Livius wrote tragedies and comedies and as Rome's first dramatist, started from scratch – he adapted Greek plays into Latin, thereby establishing the form of both genres, built the stage and set, and performed in his own plays until his voice gave out, which led him to introduce singers who sang *cantica* off stage while he gesticulated on stage. This suggests that Livius had diminished the role of the chorus in favour of *cantica*, sung by characters, thereby changing Greek trimeters (conversational meter) into Latin *septenarii* and *octonarii* (song meters). This change affected the architecture of the Roman theatre, since an orchestra was not necessary if actors, rather than the chorus, provided the lyrical component of the drama. In recognition of Livius' literary accomplishments, he was selected to compose the Partheneion of 207 BCE, in gratitude for which the Temple of Minerva on the Aventine was dedicated as the site of a writer's guild (*collegium poetarum*) in his honor.

Naevius was Italian born and served in the First Punic War (264-241 BCE). He presented his first tragedy in 235 BCE (only five years after Livius' first play) and thus emerges as the first native Italian dramatist. Naevius earned a reputation for outspokenness off the stage (Aulus Gellius refers to his *superbia Campana, N.A.* 3.3). Apparently, in connection with an offense against the Metelli he was imprisoned and exiled, but this account may be fictional.[5] It is difficult to imagine that Naevius was not a member of Livius' audience, since he follows Livius' innovative lead in dramatic format and language. As a soldier in the First Punic War, however, Naevius may also have come into contact with Greek tragedy in southern Italy. Naevius showed originality by introducing the *fabula praetexta*, or historical drama in Roman dress, at Rome. Unfortunately, not many fragments survive from Naevius' tragedies and comedies. The problem of reconstructing the plays is made more complicated by the fact that it is difficult to separate Nae-

---

4   Extant titles of tragedies: *Achilles; Aegisthus; Ajax Mastigophorus; Andromeda; Danae; Equos Troianus; Hermiona; Ino(?); Tereus.*

5   Naevius' apparent insult against the Metelli: *Fato Metelli Romae consules fiunt,* earned the response: *Dabunt malum Metelli Naevio poetae,* referring to Naevius' supposed imprisonment.

vius' fragments and even titles of his plays from those of Livius, due to the proximity in date and similarities in language and versification which later audiences/readers could not distinguish.[6]

Naevius' *Bellum Punicum* was the first verse history of Rome and as such anticipated Cato's *Origines,* which was the first Latin prose history. The grammarian C. Octavius Lampadio divided the *Bellum Punicum* into seven books (Naevius had not divided his poem into books). It is significant for later epic (Ennius and Vergil) that Naevius incorporated mythological material into his narrative of remote and contemporary historical events, from the fall of Troy to the end of the First Punic War. Readers of the *Aeneid,* however, may be surprised to find alternate versions of the Aeneas myth in the *Bellum Punicum.* Naevius narrates the fall of Troy, the departure of Aeneas and Anchises, and perhaps their wives, a possible stop-over in Carthage, the arrival of both Aeneas and Anchises in Italy, and states that Romulus, the grandson of Aeneas, founded Rome. Even though these versions contradict much of the *Aeneid*'s narrative, Vergil based several passages of Aeneas' wanderings on the *Bellum Punicum.*

In addition to mythological content, Hellenistic literary techniques are also present, such as *aitia* and a *sphragis,* or poet's seal, by which a self-conscious poet leaves a literary thumb-print in his poem, demonstrating that Naevius was aware of contemporary Greek literary innovations. Despite his study of these recent Greek innovations, however, Naevius chose to compose his epic in Saturnians. As with Livius, it is difficult to imagine how Naevius, who incorporated Greek meters into his tragedies and comedies, could not have composed hexameter verse had he so wished, especially since he composed his epic in old age after establishing a reputation as a dramatist. It would seem that a conscious decision was made to use an Italic meter for Italic subject matter. Naevius' remarkable achievements were recognized by Cicero, who compared his poetry to a work by the Greek artist Myron – brilliant yet not perfect (*Brutus* 19.75).

Ennius was born in Calabria, a region with strong Greek, Roman, and Oscan cultural traditions. Cato brought Ennius to Rome from Sardinia, where he had been serving as a soldier. In Rome, the consul M. Fulvius Nobilior soon became his patron and asked Ennius to form part of his personal train, in the Hellenistic tradition, on his Aetolian Campaign, the war celebrated in the *Annales.* The first hexameter poem written in Rome, the *Annales* was originally composed in fifteen books, and covered events from Aeneas' departure from Troy to the Aetolian campaign of his patron M. Fulvius Nobilior. Ennius added three more books at a later date and fragments from all eighteen books survive. Following Naevius' lead, Ennius incorporated mythological material into his contemporary historical epic, but he omitted

---

6 Extant titles of tragedies: *Danae; Equos Troianus* (cf. Livius*); Hector Proficiscens; Hesione; Iphegenia; Lycurgus;* and the *fabulae praetextae: Clastidium* and *Romulus sive Lupus.*

a description of the First Carthaginian War (and possibly the wanderings of
Aeneas), since Naevius had already written about it in the *Bellum Punicum*.
Like Naevius, Ennius made Romulus a grandson of Aeneas. The *Annales*
was highly influential to later poets and we find the distinct marks of it
throughout Vergil's *Aeneid*.

Ennius begins the *Annales* with a dream (in the Hesiodic tradition) in
which Homer was first turned into a peacock, as a vehicle for his metem-
psychosis (or reincarnation) as Ennius. This image is bold, since Ennius
through Homer is presenting the first Latin hexameter poem. In appealing
to Homer and his hexameter verse, Ennius thereby distances himself from
his Latin precursors Livius and Naevius as he makes clear in the proem (or
preface) from *Annales* Book 7:

> *scripsere alii rem*
> *vorsibus quos olim Faunei vatesque canebant*
> (Skutsch, **i)

> *[cum] neque Musarum scopulos [...]*
> *nec dicti studiosus [quisquam erat] ante hunc*

> *Nos ausi reserare [...]*
> (Skutsch, **ia)

Ennius derides Livius and Naevius as *vates* with its earlier meaning, not
of poets, but of soothsayers and quacks who made utterances in preliterate
carmen and Saturnian verse. This stance contrasts with his own as a modern
Hellenized *poeta,* signalled by the expression *dicti studiosus*, and results in
a dual and competing claim for founding Latin verse based on the Hellenic
hexameter rather than the Italic Saturnian verse. To the victor go the spoils,
and Ennius made much of his literary triumph at the expense of his precursors
who had laid much of the groundwork in establishing Latin poetry.

Ennius wrote his tragedies and comedies concurrently with his *Annales*.
The titles of 21 tragedies are known, and the fragments reveal an innova-
tive flair; but an excellent command of *carmen*-style verse techniques is
also present, despite the Hellenic and Hellenistic posturings in his epic
and his antagonism against the Saturnians of Livius and Naevius.[7] Ennius,
for example, adopts the dramatic format and archaizing vocabulary of his
precursors, thus adding an archaic patina to tragedy that was to influence
his successors Pacuvius and Accius. Ennius' last play, the *Thyestes*, was
performed in 169 BCE, the year of his death.

---

7 Extant titles of Ennius' tragedies: *Achilles* (cf. Livius); *Ajax* (cf. Livius?);
Alcmeo; Alexander; Andromache sive Andromache Aechmalotis; Andromeda
(cf. Livius); *Athamas; Chresphontes; Erectheus; Eumenides; Hectoris Lytra;
Hecuba; Iphegenia in Aulis* (cf. Naevius); *Medea Exul; Melanippa; Nemea;
Phoenix; Telephus; Thyestes;* and the *praetextae: Ambracia* and *Sabinae*.

In addition to the well-known plays of Plautus and Terence, comedy was first written at Rome by Livius, Naevius, Ennius, and Caecilius Statius (later by Accius and others), but their plays, with the exception of those of Caecilius Statius, were eclipsed by the plays of Plautus and, later, Terence. Plautus wrote comedies (130 were later attributed to him) in the burlesque, slapstick manner. Terence, however, aimed for linguistic and stylistic "purity" with his Greek originals and preferred a more sophisticated style in the six plays that he wrote. The comedies of Plautus contain polymetric arias, which the plays of Terence do not. The most peculiar feature of Terence's comedies is the inclusion of an audience address which was read by his stage manager. In these, we get a glimpse of the audience's reactions to his plays (unfavourable), and his own defense of his art.

Caecilius Statius' plays were enormously successful for their plots, emotional power, and a certain *gravitas* admired later by Horace. The titles from 42 plays are known, 16 of which are adaptations of plays by Menander. Caecilius flourished in the first third of the second century BCE and died in 168 BCE. Caecilius' *Plocium* is an adaptation of Menander's *Plokion*. Aulus Gellius (*N.A.* 2.23.1-22) compares selections from each play and draws the conclusion that Caecilius' play would be considered a success had Menander's original not survived to prove superior. It is clear from Aulus Gellius' discussion, however, that Caecilius did not attempt a literal translation, since he often compresses the Greek into fewer lines, changes the context to suit a Roman audience, weeds out Greek references that would have made little sense to Romans, and adds a farcical element, in places, not found in the Greek.

Roman tragedy reached its peak under Pacuvius and Accius. Pacuvius, born in 220 BCE in Brundisium, was Ennius' nephew. Pacuvius was the only early writer who composed tragedies exclusively, and he also achieved fame as a painter.[8] Extant fragments reveal an interest in the psychology of his characters and the use of vocabulary and syntax to complement characterization. Accius was a prolific tragedian, and fragments from 46 titled plays survive.[9] Accius also approached his tragedies with a similar sophistic approach. As the author of numerous literary genres, like Ennius before him, Accius was interested in questions of orthography. Accius was the first to write a history of Latin literature in his *Didaskalia*, and he also

---

8 Pacuvius' extant titles: *Antiopa; Armorum Iudicium; Atalanta; Chryses; Dulorestes; Hermione* (cf. Livius); *Iliona; Medus; Niptra; Pentheus* (cf. Naevius' *Lycurgus*?); *Periboea; Teucer*; and the *fabula praetexta: Paullus*.

9 Extant titles of Accius' tragedies: *Achilles/Myrmidones* (cf. Livius, Ennius); *Agamemnonidae/Erigona; Alcmeo/Alphesiboea* (cf. Ennius); *Amphitryo* (cf. Plautus); *Andromeda; Antenoridae; Antigona; Armorum Iudicium* (cf. Pacuvius); *Astyanax/Troades; Athamas; Atreus; Bacchae; Chrysippus; Clytaemestra/Aegisthus* (cf. Livius); *Deiphobus; Diomedes; Epigoni/Eriphyle*(?); *Epinausimache; Eurysaces; Hellenes* (?); *Liberi* (cf. Naevius'

wrote an *Annales* in hexameter, but the subject matter is unknown. Accius was born in 170 BCE in Pisaurum and was a friend of Pacuvius, with whom he was also a literary rival (they both presented plays at the same festival when Accius was 30 and Pacuvius was 80). Accius enjoyed the patronage of Brutus Callaicus for whom he wrote the *praetexta Brutus.*

Satire is a wholly Roman genre invented by Ennius, whose satires in various meters survive in very few fragments. Lucilius began writing his *Satires* in Saturnians, but abandoned the awkwardness of this meter for the more flexible hexameter (beginning with Book 30). Since the earliest books of the *Satires* (26-30) date to c.132-125 BCE, it is remarkable that Saturnian verse was still influential at such a "late" date. Lucilius (b.? – died 102/101) was from a wealthy noble family (he did not write poetry for a living), and this social position gave him access to the most influential people of Rome and may explain the fearless tone. Lucilius varied his subject matter greatly, explored literary and grammatical topics, painted scathing character sketches of various professions and provincial Italians, and adopted a candid *persona*, all of which influenced Horace and Juvenal. Many fragments contain a mixture of Latin and Greek words that reflects Lucilius' interests in lexography and literary composition, perhaps best illustrated in his trading of insults with Accius.

This brief sketch of the range and innovations of Rome's earliest writers reveals both the extent to which later writers of every genre were indebted to them, and also the need for us to understand this debt through a study of their fragments. Later writers adopted or challenged earlier versions of myths and gave their works an archaic *patina* by incorporating the vocabulary and syntax of their precursors. One cannot understand Latin poets such as Vergil only through comparisons with Homer and other Greek poets. As the fragments of Livius, Naevius, and Ennius reveal, Vergil's audience would have also heard throughout his epic the echo of an earlier poetry, however faint to us today, that is decidedly Italian/Roman.

Lycurgus); *Medea/Argonautae* (cf. Ennius); *Meleager; Minos/Minotaurus; Neoptolemus; Nyctegressia; Oenomaus; Pelopidae; Philocteta/Philocteta Lemnius; Phinidae; Phoenissae; Prometheus (?); Stasiastae/Tropaeum* (cf. Naevius' *Lycurgus?*); *Telephus; Tereus; Thebais* (?); and the *praetextae: Brutus* and *Aeneadae sive Decius.*

I. ORAL POETRY

I. *Carmina*

1.   ego tui memini,   1
     medere meis pedibus;
     terra pestem teneto,
     salus hic maneto
     in meis pedibus.   5
     (Varro, *R.R.* 1.2.27)

2.   novum vetus vinum bibo   1
     novo veteri morbo medeor.
     (Varro, *L.L.* 6.21)

3.   hiberno pulvere verno luto   1
     grandia farra, camille, metes.
     (Macrobius, *Sat.* 5.20.18)

4.   Mars pater, te precor quaesoque   1
     uti sies volens propitius
     mihi domo familiaeque nostrae;
     quoius rei ergo
     agrum terram fundumque meum   5
     suovitaurilia circumagi iussi;
     uti tu morbos visos invisosque
     viduertatem vastitudinemque calamitates intemperiasque
     prohibessis defendas averruncesque;
     utique tu fruges frumenta vineta virgultaque   10
     grandire beneque evenire siris,
     pastores pecuaque salva servassis
     duisque bonam salutem valetudinemque
     mihi domo familiaeque nostrae.
     harumce rerum ergo   15
     fundi terrae agrique mei

lustrandi lustrique faciendi ergo,
sicuti dixi,
macte hisce suovitaurilibus lactentibus immolandis esto.
Mars pater, eiusdem rei ergo   20
macte hisce suovitaurilibus lactentibus esto.
(Cato, *de Agr.* 141)

II. *Versus Populares*

1. Postquam Crassus carbo factus, Carbo crassus factus est.
    (Sacerd. p. 461 K)

2. Brutus, quia reges eiecit, consul primus factus est:
    Hic, quia consules eiecit, rex postremus factus est.
    (Suet. *Jul. 80.3)*

3. Rex erit qui recte faciet; qui non faciet, non erit.
    (Porph. *ad Hor. Sat. 1.1.62)*

4. Gallias Caesar subegit, Nicomedes Caesarem.
    ecce Caesar nunc triumphat qui subegit Gallias
    Nicomedes non triumphat qui sebegit Caesarem.
    (Suet. *Jul.* 49)

II. VERSE EPITAPHS

The following inscriptions are some of the many epitaphs from the funeral monument of the Scipios found near the Via Appia. Inscription 1 is the earliest in date, yet the inscription is a reworking of the original, based on modern spellings and later Hellenizing concepts, of which the first line is still preserved. The second epitaph is more recent in date than the first, yet it incorporates archaisms to give the impression that it is as old as the original inscription of the first one. Both are written in approximation throughout to Saturnians. Epitaph 3 is from the mid-second century BCE, yet it retains the meter and features from third century BCE inscriptions. Soon after the date of this epitaph, the elegiac meter was used in tomb inscriptions, of which the fourth inscription is perhaps the earliest surviving example.

1. Lucius Cornelius Scipio Barbatus (consul 298, censor 290 BCE).[10]

   a) [L. Cornelio] Cn. f. Scipio   1

   b) Cornelius Lucius Scipio Barbatus   1
      Gnaivod patre prognatus, fortis vir sapiensque,
      quoius forma virtutei parisuma fuit,
      consol censor aidilis quei fuit apud vos,
      Taurasia Cisauna Samnio cepit   5
      subigit omne Loucanam opsidesque abdoucit.

2. Lucius Cornelius Scipio (consul 259, censor 258 BCE).

   a) [L.] Cornelio L.f. Scipio   1
      [a]idiles cosol cesor

   b) Honc oino ploirume cosentiont R[omai]   1
      duonoro optumo fuise viro,
      Luciom Scipione. Filios Barbati
      consol censor aidilis hic fuet a[pud vos].

---

10 Texts from E.H. Warmington, (*ROL* IV) 2-8.

    hec cepit Corsica Aleriaque urbe   5
    dedet Tempestatebus aide mereto[d].

3. Lucius Cornelius Scipio (about 160?).

    L. Cornelius Cn. f. Cn. n. Scipio   1
    Magna sapientia multasque virtutes
    aetate quom parva posidet hoc saxsum.
    Quoiei vita defecit, non honos, honore,
    is hic situs, quei nunquam victus est virtutei,   5
    annos gnatus XX is l[oc]eis mandatus.
    Ne quairatis honore quei minus sit mandatus.

4. Gnaeus Cornelius Scipio Hispanus (praetor peregrinus 139 BCE).

    Cn. Cornelius Cn. f. Scipio Hispanus pr. aid. cur.   1
        q. tr. mil. II Xvir sl. iudik. Xvir sacr. fac.

    Virtutes generis mieis moribus accumulavi,
        progeniem genui, facta patris petiei.
    Maiorum optenui laudem, ut sibei me esse creatum   5
        laetentur; stirpem nobilitavit honor.

III. EPIC I – SATURNIAN VERSE

I. Livius Andronicus

Odyssia
(Selections)

Book 1

1 (1). Virum mihi, Camena, insece versutum.[11]

2 (2). Pater noster, Saturni filie...

3 (3). Mea puer, quid verbi ex tuo ore supera fugit?

4 (4). argenteo polubro, aureo eclutro.

5 (5). tuque mihi narrato omnia disertim.

6 (6). quae haec daps est, qui festus dies, ...?

7 (7). matrem <proci> procitum plurimi venerunt.

Book 2

1 (9). tumque remos iussit religare struppis

Book 3

1 (10). ibidemque vir summus adprimus Patroclus

2 (11). quando dies adveniet, quem profata Morta est

---

11 Fragments cited from W. Morel, 7-17. Morel's fragment numbers appear in parentheses.

Book 4

1 (13). partim errant, nequinont Graeciam redire.

2 (14). Sancta puer, Saturni filia, regina

3 (15). apud nympham Atlantis filiam Calypsonem

Book 5

1 (16). igitur demum Ulixi cor frixit prae pavore

Book 6

1 (17). utrum genua amploctens virginem oraret

2 (18). ibi manens sedeto donicum videbis
me carpento vehentem domum venisse

Book 8

1 (19). simul ac dacrimas de ore noegeo detersit.

2 (20). namque nullum peius macerat †humanum†
quamde mare saevom: vires cui sunt magnae,
[tamen] topper confringent importunae undae.

3 (21). Mercurius cumque eo filius Latonas

4 (23). Nam diva Monetas filia docuit

Book 10

1 (25). Inferus an superus tibi fert deus funera, Ulixes?

2 (26). Topper citi ad aedis venimus Circae

Book 19

1 (30). vestis pulla purpurea ampla...

Book 20

1 (32). cum socios nostros mandisset impius Cyclops

Book 21

1 (34). inque manum suremit hastam...

Book 22

1 (35). At celer hasta volans perrumpit pectora ferro

Book 23

1 (36).   carnis
vinumque quod libabant anclabatur

Book 24

1 (37). deque manibus dextrabus...

II. Naevius

Bellum Punicum

Book 1

After an invocation to the Muses, the narrative seems to begin with the
Roman declaration of war against Carthage and then shifts to mythological
material surrounding Aeneas' departure from Troy for the remote cause(s)
of the first Punic War.

1.   Novem Iovis concordes filiae sorores... [12]

2*.   Scopas atque verbenas sagmina sumpserunt.

3.   Manius Valerius
        Consul partem exerciti in expeditionem
        ducit...

4.   Inerant signa expressa, quomodo Titani,
        bicorpores Gigantes magnique Atlantes
        Runcus ac Purpureus, filii Terras...

5*.   amborum uxores
        noctu Troiad exibant capitibus opertis
        flentes ambae, abeuntes lacrimis cum multis...

6.   eorum sectam sequuntur multi mortales [...]
        multi alii e Troia strenui viri [...]
        ubi foras cum auro illi[n]c exibant

7.   [Serv. Dan. *ad Aen.* 1.170: *novam...rem Naevius bello
        Punico dicit, unam navem habuisse Aenean, quam Mercurius
        fecerit.*]

8*.   res divas edicit, praedicit castus...

---

12 The text is from W. Strzelecki, 1-29. I retain Strzelecki's numbering of fragments
    which includes an asterix to denote that a passage survives without a specific
    book attribution.

9*.   [Schol. *ad Aen.* 7.123: *N(a)evius... dicit Venerem libros futura continentes Anchis(a)e dedisse.*]

10*. Senex fretus pietati deum adlocutus
      summi deum regis fratrem Neptunum
      regnatorem marum...

11.   Silvicolae homines bellique inertes...

12*. [Lact. *Div.inst.* 1.6.9: *quartam (sc. Sibyllam) Cimeriam in Italia, quam Naevius in libris belli Punici, Piso in annalibus nominet.*]

13.   [Serv. Dan. *ad Aen.* 9.712, re: Prochyta: *...hanc Naevius in primo belli Punici de cognata Aeneae nomen accepisse dicit.*]

14.   [Macrob. *Sat.* 6.2.31: *In principio Aeneidos tempestas describitur et Venus apud Iovem queritur de periculis filii et Iuppiter eam de futurorum prosperitate solatur. Hic locus totus sumptus a Naevio est ex primo libro Belli Punici. Illic enim aeque Venus Troianis tempestate laborantibus cum Iove queritur et secuntur verba Iovis filiam consolantis spe futurorum.*]

15*. [Serv. Dan. *ad Aen* 1.198: *O socii... et totus hic locus de Naevio belli Punici libro translatus est.*]

16.   Ei venit in mentem hominum fortunas...

17*. patrem suum supremum optumum appellat...

18*. Summe deum regnator, quianam genus [od]isti?

Book 2

The narrative of Aeneas' adventures following his departure from Troy continues.

19.   Prima incedit Cereris Proserpina puer...

20.   dein pollens sagittis inclutus arquitenens
      sanctus Iove prognatus Pythius Apollo.

21*. [Serv. Dan. *ad Aen* 4.9: *Anna soror cuius filiae fuerint Anna et Dido, Naevius dicit.*]

22*. pulcraque [vasa] ex auro vestemque citrosam...

23.   blande et docte percontat, Aenea quo pacto
      Troiam urbem liquerit [...]

24.   Iamque eius mentem fortuna fecerat quietem.

Book 3

Book 3 seems to cover the period from Aeneas' arrival in Italy to events surrounding the founding of Rome.

25. Postquam avem aspexit in templo Anchisa,
     sacra in mensa penatium ordine ponuntur;
     immolabat auream victimam pulchram.

26. manusque susum ad caelum sustulit suas rex
     Amulius divis[que] gratulabatur...

27*. [Serv. Dan. *ad Aen.* 1.273: [*Donec regina sacerdos*]...*Naevius et
     Ennius Aeneae ex filia nepotem Romulum conditorem urbis
     tradunt.*]

28*. [Varro, *de lingua Latina* 5.53: *Eundem hunc locum (sc. Palatium)
     a pecore dictum putant quidam; itaque N(a)evius "Balatium"
     appellat.*]

29*. [Varro, *de lingua Latina* 5.43: *Aventinum aliquot de causis dicunt.
     N(a)evius ab avibus, quod eo se ab Tiberi ferent aves...*]

Book 4

An account of the first Punic War begins.

30*. [Fest. 162a O.M. (156 L): <*Navali corona*>...
     Atillus bel<lo> ....*tum est in car<mine>.*]

31*. [Prisc. G.L.K. II 249,3: *"hic" et "haec Samnis huius Samnitis"
     ... huius neutrum Naevius Samnite protulit in carmine belli Pu-
     nici.*]

32. Transit Melitam
     Romanus exercitus, insulam integram urit,
     populatur, vastat, rem hostium concinnat.

33. simul atrocia proicerent exta ministratores...

34. virum praetor adveneit, auspicat auspicium
     prosperum...

35. eam carnem victoribus danunt...

36. vicissatim volvi victoriam...

Book 5

No fragments can be assigned to Book 5.

Book 6

Possibly covering Roman activities in Sicily.

37. Superbiter contemtim conterit legiones...

38. Convenit, regnum simul atque locos ut haberent...

39.   septimum decimum annum ilico sedent...

40.   censet eo venturum obviam Poenum...

Book 7

The narrative covers C. Lutatius Catulus' naval victory at the Aegates Islands and the Peace settlement of 241 BCE.

41*.   Onerariae onustae stabant in flustris...

42*.   Silicienses paciscit obsides ut reddant...

43.   id quoque paciscunt, † moenia sint quae
      Lutatium reconciliant captivos plurimos †

44*.   [Gell. N.A. 17.21.45: ... *eodemque anno Cn. Naevius poeta Fabulas apud populum dedit, quem M. Varro in libro de poetis Primo stipendia fecisse ait bello Poenico primo idque ipsum Naevium dicere in eo carmine, quod de eodem bello scripsit.*]

Fragmenta Incertae Sedis[13]

58   cum tu arquitenens, sagittis pollens Dea<na>

---

13 For other fragments from unknown books, see Strzelecki, 22-27.

IV. TRAGEDY I

Livius Andronicus

Aegisthus

Eight fragments survive from the *Aegisthus,* yet it is unclear whether Livius used Aeschylus' *Agamemnon,* Sophocles' *Aegisthus,* or some other play as a model. The dramatic action centers around the return of Agamemnon, with Cassandra, to Mycenae after the fall of Troy, his murder and Aegisthus' subsequent usurpation of power.

Fragments 1 and 2 describe the fall of Troy and the voyage from Troy:

1.   nam ut Pergama
    accensa et praeda per participes aequiter
    partita est. [14]

2.   Tum autem lascivum Nerei simum pecus
    ludens ad cantum classum lustratur ...

Fragment 3 refers to the addressee as a stock stage-tyrant, overstepping the bounds of nature and civilization, through a gluttonous appetite for pleasure or power:

3.   Iamne oculos specie laetavisti optabili?

Fragments 4 and 5 describe the return of Agamemnon and Cassandra to Mycenae:

4.   Nemo haec vostrorum ruminetur mulieri.

5.   Sollemnitus deo litat laudem lubens.

---

14 Quoted are the texts and fragment numbers as they appear in Otto Ribbeck, (TRF), 1-2. As with all extant fragments from Roman tragedy, the exact placement of the fragments within the play must remain conjectural.

Details surrounding the murder of Agamemnon:

6.   ... in sedes conlocat se regias:
       Clytemestra iuxtim; tertias natae occupant.

7.   Ipsus se in terram saucius fligit cadens.

In fragment 8, Aegisthus behaves like a tyrant (ordering Electra?):

8.   Quin quod parere <mihi> vos maiestas mea
       procat, toleratis temploque hanc deducitis?

With the death of Agamemnon, Aegisthus and Clytemnestra emerge triumphant at the end of the play.

Tereus

The Greek model for Livius' *Tereus* is unknown but the story is famous from Ovid's *Metamorphoses* (6.412-674). Tereus rapes his wife's sister Philomela and mutilates her to prevent her from telling Procne, her sister. Procne discovers Tereus' crime, however, and exacts revenge by serving him his own son, Itys.

The context of the first fragment is unclear:

1.   rarenter venio.[15]

In the second surviving fragment, does Tereus realize he has eaten his son?

2.   nimis pol impudenter: servis praestolabas?

Fragments 3 and 4 reveal Procne's knowledge of Tereus' crime through her plotting of revenge (by fattening of the sacrificial child), and Philomela's (?) defence of her character to person(s) unknown:

3.   ego puerum interea ancillae subdam lactentem meae,
       ne fame perbitat.

4.   credito,
       cum illoc olli mea voluntate numquam limavit caput.

The play's ending may have alluded to the subsequent metamorphoses of Procne into a swallow, Philomela into a nightingale, and Tereus into a hawk.

---

15 Quoted are the texts and fragment numbers from Otto Ribbeck (TRF), 4.

Naevius

Danae

The Greek model(s) of the *Danae* is unknown but possible plays include Sophocles' *Acrisius, Danae* (?), and *Men of Larissa*; and Euripides' *Danae*. One cannot rule out that Livius' *Danae* may also have been influential. The basic outline of the myth is as follows: Acrisius, fearing an oracle that a grandchild would kill him, imprisoned his daughter Danae, who was loved by Jupiter in the form of gold. Danae and her son, Perseus, were locked in a chest, put out to sea, and drifted until they finally reached Seriphus. Eleven fragments from Naevius' *Danae* survive but they are difficult to place within the dramatic action of the play, which seems to center around events following the rape of Danae when Acrisius punishes her with imprisonment and exile for the birth of Perseus.

A reference to Jupiter?/Acrisius?

1.   omnes formidant homines eius valentiam.[16]

Fragment 2 defends or mocks Danae's current/former character:

2.   contempla placide formam et faciem virginis.

A description of Danae?

3.   excidit orationis omnis confidentia.

Acrisius accusing Danae of promiscuity?

4.   eam compotem scis nunc esse inventam probri.

Danae recounts how Jupiter seduced her:

5.   amnis niveo fonte lavere <me> memini manum.

Danae complaining of the unfair treatment of women, or Acrisius fearing gossip about Danae's pregnancy?

6.   desubito famam tollunt, si quam solam videre in via.

Acrisius justifies his punishment of Danae:

7.   quin, ut quisque est meritus, praesens pretium pro factis ferat.

Danae protests her innocence:

8.   ... indigne exigor patria innocens

---

16 Quoted are the texts and fragment numbers from Otto Ribbeck, (TRF), 7-9.

9.   quamne quondam fulmine icit Iuppiter.

Danae beseeches Jupiter for help?

10.   manubias suppetiat prone...

Jupiter responds?

11.   suo sonitu claro fulgorivit Iuppiter.

Lycurgus

The Greek model(s) of the *Lycurgus* is difficult to recover. Possible plays include one or more from Aeschylus' tetralogy *Lycourgeia,* and Euripides' *Bacchae.* Later, Accius' *Stasiastae* included a chorus of Lycurgus' followers, which may have been influenced by Naevius' play. The basic outline of the play is as follows: Maenads and Liber arrive in Thrace only to meet resistance and imprisonment from Lycurgus, who is eventually punished by Liber. A relatively large number of fragments have survived.

Fragments 1-4 describe the arrival of the Maenads:

1.   tuos qui celsos terminos tutant...[17]

2.   alte iubatos angues in sese gerunt.

3.   Liberi <sunt>: quaque incedunt, omnis arvas opterunt.

4.   suavisonum melus.

In fragments 5 and 6, Lycurgus orders the capture of the Maenads:

5.   Vos, qui regalis corporis custodias
      agitatis, ite actutum in frundiferos locos,
      ingenio arbusta ubi nata sunt, non obsita.

6.   ducite
      eo cum argutis linguis mutas quadrupedis.

The Maenads are described as birds as they flee Lycurgus' guards:

7.   <alias> alis
      sublime in altos saltus inlicite <invios>,
      ubi bipedes volucres lino linquant lumina.

8.   Ut in venatu vitulantis ex suis
      lucis nos mittat poenis decoratos feris?

_____

17 Quoted are the text and fragment numbers from Otto Ribbeck, (TRF), 10-15.

9.   pergite,
    tyrsigerae Bacchae, Bacchico cum schemate.

10.   Ignotae iteris sumus: tute scis...

Lycurgus speaks:

11.   Dic quo pacto eum potiti: pugnan an dolis?

Fragments 12-16 describe Liber's confrontation with Lycurgus:

12.   Ne ille mei feri ingeni <iram> atque animi acrem acrimoniam

Liber warns Lycurgus:

13.   Cave sis tuam contendas iram contra cum ira Liberi.

Liber speaks the first half of the line, Lycurgus the second:

14.   Oderunt di homines iniuros.- Egone an ille iniurie
       facimus?

Liber speaks?

15.   Sic quasi amnis celeris rapit, sed tamen inflexu flectitur.

16.   Iam ibi nos duplicat advenientis ... timos pavos.

The guards approach Liber and the Maenads:

17.   Namque ludere ut laetantis inter sese vidimus
       propter amnem, aquam creterris sumere ex fonte...

18.   Pallis patagiis crocotis malacis mortualibus

19.   sine terrore pecua ut ad mortem meant.

Liber exacts his revenge against Lycurgus:

20.   ...ut videam Volcani opera haec flammis fieri flora.

21.   Proinde huc Dryante regem prognatum patre,
       Lycurgum cette!

22.   Iam solis aestu candor cum liquesceret

23.   late longeque transtros nostros fervere.

24.   Vos, qui astatis obstinati...

                    Incerti Nominis Reliquiae

4.   diabathra in pedibus habebat, erat amictus epicroco.

Ennius

Alexander

The Greek model of the *Alexander* was either the *Alexander* of Euripides or the *Alexander* of Sophocles. The dramatic action of the play seems to have been the source for Hyginus' summary of the myth of Alexander, making a plot outline of the play possible to reconstruct.[18] The action of the play revolves around Priam's acknowledgement of his son Alexander (Paris). Alexander was exposed at birth and raised by herdsmen on Mount Ida. Years later, at the games given by Priam to commemorate Alexander's death, Alexander, disguised as a shepherd, defeated and angered Hector and Deiphobus in a contest, causing Deiphobus to plot his murder. Cassandra, however, reveals Alexander's true identity and he is accepted into the family before Deiphobus can act on his anger. Thirteen fragments of Ennius' play survive. The exact placement of the fragments is uncertain in many instances, but the context of Cassandra's speeches is preserved by Cicero.[19]

> Fragments 1-4 describe Cassandra's prophesies about Alexander, whose identity has probably been revealed to the audience but not to the characters on stage:

1.   sed quid oculis rapere visa est derepente ardentibus?
       Ubi illa paulo ante sapiens †virginali† modestia?

       mater, optumatum multo mulier melior mulierum,
       missa sum superstitiosis hariolationibus;
       †neque† me Apollo fatis fandis dementem invitam ciet.
       Virgines vereor aequalis, patris mei meum factum pudet,
       optumi viri. mea mater, tui me miseret, mei piget.
       Optumam progeniem Priamo peperisti extra me. hoc dolet:
       men obesse, illos prodesse, me obstare, illos obsequi.
       (Jocelyn, 33-40)

2.   adest adest fax obvoluta sanguine atque incendio.
       Multos annos latuit. Cives ferte opem et restinguite.
       (Jocelyn, 41-42)

3.   iamque mari magno classis cita

---

18 Hyginus, *Fab.* 91. On Hyginus' use of Ennius' play, see H. D. Jocelyn *The Tragedies of Ennius* (Cambridge, 1967), 202, n. 2; Warmington, I, 234.

19 Quoted is the text of Jocelyn, 75-81, with corresponding line numbers in parentheses. Jocelyn (202-234) discusses the dramatic and linguistic context of these fragments fully. For other texts of the fragments, see Ribbeck, (TRF), 19-22, and Warmington, (*ROL* I), 234-245.

texitur. Exitium examen rapit.
Adveniet. fera velivolantibus
navibus complevit manus litora.
(Jocelyn, 43-46)

4.   eheu videte:
iudicavit inclitum iudicium inter deas tris aliquis,
quo iudicio Lacedaemonia mulier Furiarum una adveniet.
(Jocelyn, 47-49)

The exact placement of fragment 5 is unclear, but it describes another of Cassandra's visions and the necessary expiatory rites:

5.   mater gravida parere se ardentem facem
visa est in somnis Hecuba. quo facto pater
rex ipse Priamus somnio mentis metu
perculsus curis sumptus suspirantibus
exsacrificabat hostiis balantibus.
tum coniecturam postulat pacem petens,
ut se edoceret obsecrans Apollinem
quo sese vertant tantae sortes somnium.
ibi ex oraclo voce divina edidit
Apollo puerum primus Priam qui foret
postilla natus temperaret tollere;
eum esse exitium Troiae, pestem Pergamo.
(Jocelyn, 50-61)

Fragment 6 refers to the games given by Priam in honour of Alexander:

6.   iam dudum ab ludis animus atque aures auent
avide exspectantes nuntium.
(Jocelyn, 62-63)

The etymology of Alexander's name is referred to in the next fragment:

7.   quapropter Parim pastores nunc Alexandrum vocant.
(Jocelyn, 64)

The contexts of fragments 8 and 9 are unclear:

8.   †amidio† purus put<us>
(Jocelyn, 65)

9.   Hominem appellat.'quid †lascivi† stolide?'non intellegit.
(Jocelyn, 66)

Fragment 10 refers to Alexander's victory at the games, but it is unclear whether the line comes from a messenger speech or whether it actually comes from the prologue of the play spoken by Victory:

10.   volans de caelo cum corona et taeniis.
      (Jocelyn, 67)

A description of the games is given in fragment 11:

11.   multi alii adventant, paupertas quorum obscurat nomina.
      (Jocelyn, 68)

Fragments 12 and 13 describe Cassandra's visions of Alexander's future:

12.   o lux Troiae, germane Hector,
      quid ita cum tuo lacerato corpore miser?
      aut qui te sic respectantibus tractavere nobis?
      (Jocelyn, 69-71)

13.   nam maximo saltu superavit gravidus armatis equus
      qui suo partu ardua perdat Pergama.
      (Jocelyn, 72-73)

Medea Exul

The *Medea Exul* is based upon the *Medea* of Euripides, in which Medea, hearing of Jason's marriage to Creon's daughter, plans her revenge by killing his bride, murdering her children, and fleeing to Athens. It is very likely that Ennius wrote a second play about Medea, called *Medea*, based on Euripides' *Aigeus*, whose action is set in Athens after the events at Corinth took place. It is doubtful that Ennius would have combined all the events of Corinth and Athens into one play.[20] The fragments which survive provide valuable insights into Ennius' dramaturgy, especially on the matter of his play's relationship to Euripides' original.

Fragment 1 is a speech by Medea's Nurse (in trimeters/*senarii):*

1.   utinam ne in nemore Pelio securibus
      caesa accidisset abiegna ad terram trabes,
      neve inde navis inchoandi exordium
      cepisset, quae nunc nominatur nomine
      Argo, quia Argivi in ea delecti viri
      vecti petebant pellem inauratam arietis
      Colchis, imperio regis Peliae, per dolum.
      Nam numquam era errans mea domo efferret pedem
      Medea animo aegro amore saevo saucia.
      (Jocelyn, 208-216)[21]

---

20   Jocelyn (1967), 343-350 examines fully the question of a second *Medea* set in Athens.

2.   quo nunc me vortam? quod iter incipiam ingredi?
      domum paternamne? anne ad Peliae filias?
      (Jocelyn, 217-218)

3.   [Quae Corinthum arcem altam habetis matronae
                  opulentae optimates,]
      multi suam rem bene gessere et publicam patria procul;
      multi qui domi aetatem agerent propterea sunt
      improbati.
      (Jocelyn, 219-220)

Fragment 4 comes from the dialogue between Creon and Medea, in which
Medea tries to allay Creon's fear of her:

4.   qui ipse sibi sapiens prodesse non quit nequiquam
      sapit.
      (Jocelyn, 221)

In fragment 5, the Nurse talks about Medea's misery:

5.   cupido cepit misera nunc me proloqui
      caelo atque terrae Medeai miserias.
      (Jocelyn, 222-223)

Fragments 6-10 refer to the scene in which Medea confronts Jason about
his imminent marriage to Creon's daughter and his betrayal of their own
implicit marriage bond. Jason speaks fragment 6.

6.   tu me amoris magis quam honoris servavisti gratia
      (Jocelyn, 224)

In fragments 7-9, Medea informs the Chorus of the significance of her
conversation, which has just ended, with Jason (or Creon?) and alludes
to her use of their children to exact vengeance:

7.   nequaquam istuc istac ibit; magna inest certatio.
      Nam ut ego illi supplicarem tanta blandiloquentia
      ni ob rem —
      (Jocelyn, 225-227)

8.   qui volt quod volt ita dat <semper> se res ut operam
      dabit.
      (Jocelyn, 228)

9.   ille traversa mente mi hodie tradidit repagula

---

21 Cited is the text of Jocelyn, 113-123, with corresponding line numbers in pa-
    rentheses. Jocelyn (342-382) discusses the dramatic and linguistic context of
    these fragments fully.

quibus ego iram omnem recludam atque illi perniciem dabo
mihi maerores, illi luctum, exitium illi, exilium mihi.
(Jocelyn, 229-231)

10.   nam ter sub armis malim vitam cernere
       quam semel modo parere.
       (Jocelyn, 232-233)

In fragment 11, the Chorus, which now knows of Medea's intention to
kill her children, prays to Jupiter after she has left the stage:

11.   Juppiter tuque adeo summe Sol qui res omnis inspicis
       quique tuo lumine mare terram caelum contines
       inspice hoc facinus prius quam fit. prohibessis scelus.
       (Jocelyn, 234-236)

The Paedagogus addresses the Nurse again, in fragment 12:

12.   antiqua erilis fida custos corporis,
       quid sic te extra aedis exanimatam eliminat?
       (Jocelyn, 237-238)

Fragment 13 is out of dramatic context here and seems to come from
Ennius' second play about Medea, which is set in Athens. The city of
Athens is pointed out to Medea:

13.   asta atque Athenas anticum opulentum oppidum
       contempla et templum Cereris ad laevam aspice.
       (Jocelyn, 239-240)

In fragment 14, Medea says goodbye to her children:

14.   salvete optima corpora.
       cette manus vestras measque accipite.
       (Jocelyn, 241-242)

The contexts and placement of fragments 14-16 are very difficult to deter-
mine. Fragment 15 contains an address to Helios, Medea's grandfather:

15.   sol qui candentem in caelo sublimat facem.
       (Jocelyn, 243)

Medea's promiscuity is mentioned in fragment 16:

16.   utinam ne umquam †mede† cordis cupido corde pedem
       extulisses.
       (Jocelyn, 244)

The context of fragment 17 is unclear:

17.   fructus verborum aures aucupant.
       (Jocelyn, 245)

V. EPIC II – HEXAMETER VERSE

Ennius

Annales
(Selections)

Book 1

After an invocation to the Muses, Book 1 covers events from Aeneas' departure from Troy to Romulus' deification.

1 (**i).   Musae quae pedibus magnum pulsatis Olympum.[22]

2 (*ii).   somno leni placidoque revinctus

3 (**iii).   visus Homerus adesse poeta.

4 (**iv).   [Lucretius, *DRN* 1.120-126:
                etsi praeterea tamen esse Acherusia templa
                        Ennius aeternis exponit versibus edens,
                quo neque permanent animae neque corpora nostra,
                sed quaedam simulacra modis pallentia miris.
                unde sibi exortam semper florentis Homeri
                commemorat speciem lacrumas effundere salsas
                coepisse et rerum naturam expandere dictis.]

---

22 Fragment selections from Otto Skutsch, 70-141 who provides a detailed analysis of these and all surviving fragments. Skutsch's fragment numbers appear in parentheses and follow this system: "It marks with an asterisk fragments assigned to a definite book by conjecture, with two asterisks those not explicitly attested as belonging to the *Annals*, and with three asterisks those which have come down without the poet's name. A dagger is added to those which are given to a book different from that attested" (p.68). Skutsch capitalizes the first letter of every line of verse, but to make these passages easier to translate I have changed these to lower case when not a new sentence .

5 (**v).   O pietas animi

6 (**ix).   memini me fiere pavom.

7 (xi).   Latos [per] populos res atque poemata nostra
                  [clara] cluebunt

8 (**xii).   Doctus†que Anchisesque Venus quem pulcra dearum
                  fari donavit, divinum pectus habere

9 (xvii).   Est locus, Hesperiam quem mortales perhibebant.

10 (**xviii).   Saturnia terra

11 (**xix).   Quam Prisci, casci populi, tenuere Latini

12 (**xx).   Saturno
                  Quem Caelus genuit

13 (**xxi).   Cum †suo obsidio magnus Titanus premebat

14 (xxii).   Teque pater Tiberine tuo cum flumine sancto

15 (**xxiv).   Assaraco natus Capys optimus isque pium ex se
                  Anchisen generat

16 (*xxv).   Quos homines quondam Laurentis terra recepit.

17 (**xxvi).   Olli respondit rex Albai Longai

18 (xxvii).   Accipe daque fidem foedusque feri bene firmum

19 (**xxix).   Et cita cum tremulis anus attulit artubus lumen.
                  Talia tum memorat lacrimans, exterrita somno:
                  'Eurydica prognata, pater quam noster amavit,
                  vires vitaque corpus meum nunc deserit omne.
                  Nam me visus homo pulcer per amoena salicta
                  et ripas raptare locosque novos. ita sola
                  postilla, germana soror, errare videbar
                  tardaque vestigare et quaerere te neque posse
                  corde capessere: semita nulla pedem stabilibat.
                  Exim compellare pater me voce videtur
                  his verbis: "o gnata, tibi sunt ante gerendae
                  aerumnae, post ex fluvio fortuna resistet."
                  Haec ecfatus pater, germana, repente recessit
                  nec sese dedit in conspectum corde cupitus,
                  quamquam multa manus ad caeli caerula templa
                  tendabam lacrumans et blanda voce vocabam.
                  Vix aegro cum corde meo me somnus reliquit.'

20 (**xxx).   cenacula maxuma caeli

21 (**xxxii).   Respondit Iuno Saturnia, sancta dearum

22 (***xxxiii). Unus erit quem tu tolles in caerula caeli templa

23 (*xxxiv).   at Ilia reddita nuptum...

24 (xxxvi).   Te†saneneta precor, Venus, te genetrix patris nostri,
                ut me de caelo visas, cognata, parumper...

25 (xxxvii).   Ilia, dia nepos, quas aerumnas tetulisti...

26 (**xli).   lupus femina feta repente

27 (xlvii).   Curantes magna cum cura tum cupientes
                regni dant operam simul auspicio augurioque;
                In †monte Remus auspicio sedet atque secundam
                solus avem servat. At Romulus pulcer in alto
                quaerit Aventino, servat genus altivolantum.
                Certabant urbem Romam Remoramne vocarent.
                Omnibus cura viris uter esset induperator.
                Exspectant veluti, consul quom mittere signum
                volt, omnes avidi spectant ad carceris oras,
                quam mox emittat pictos e faucibus currus;
                sic exspectabat populus, atque ore timebat
                rebus, utri magni victoria sit data regni.
                Interea sol albus recessit in infera noctis.
                Exin candida se radiis dedit icta foras lux,
                et simul ex alto longe pulcerrima praepes,
                laeva volavit avis. simul aureus exoritur sol
                Cedunt de caelo ter quattuor corpora sancta
                avium, praepetibus sese pulcrisque locis dant.
                Conspicit inde sibi data Romulus esse propritim,
                auspicio regni stabilita scamna solumque.

28 (xlviii).   Iuppiter ut muro fretus magis quamde manu sim.

29 (l).   Nec pol homo quisquam faciet impune animatus
              Hoc nec tu: nam mi calido dabis sanguine poenas

30 (*li).   [Schol. Bern. *Georg.* 2.384: *Romulus cum aedificasset*
              templum Iovi Feretrio, pelles unctas stravit et sic ludos
              edidit ut caestibus dimicarent et cursu contenderent,
              quam rem Ennius in Annalibus testatur.]

31 (liv).   *†Virgines nam sibi quisque domi Romanus habet sas*

32 (lvii).   Aeternum seritote diem concorditer ambo

33 (**lx).   O Tite, tute, Tati, tibi tanta, tyranne, tulisti

34 (**lxii).   Romulus in caelo cum dis genitalibus aevom
              degit

Book 2

The narrative covers the reigns of Numa Pompilius, Tullus Hostilius, and Ancus Marcius.

1 (**i).   Olli respondit suavis sonus Egeriai

2 (**ii).   Mensas constituit idemque ancilla
                Libaque, fictores, Argeos, et tutulatos

3 (**iii).   Volturnalem
                Palatualem Furinalem Floralemque
                Falacrem(que) et Pomonalem fecit hic idem

4 (iv).   Si quid me fuerit humanitus, ut teneatis

5 (**v).   Mettoeoque Fufetioeo

6 (viii).   Hic occasus datus est, at Horatius inclutus saltu

7 (**ix).   tractatus per aequora campi

8 (**x).   Volturus in †spineto† miserum mandebat homonem:
                Heu, quam crudeli condebat membra sepulcro

9 (xii).   Cael>i caerula prata

10 (xiii).   Ostia munita est. idem loca navibus pulcris
                munda facit, nautisque mari quaesentibus vitam

Book 3

Book 3 describes the reigns of the Tarquins. It is likely that the Book ended with their expulsion and the founding of the Republic.

1 (**i).   Postquam lumina sis oculis bonus Ancus reliquit

2 (ii).   Tarquinio dedit imperium simul et sola regni

3 (iii).   Et densis aquila pennis obnixa volabat
                vento quem perhibent Graium genus aera lingua

4 (vii).   Caelum prospexit stellis fulgentibus aptum

5 (viii).   Olli de caelo laevom dedit inclutus signum

6 (**ix).   Exin Tarquinium bona femina lavit et unxit

Book 4

Book 4 covers events surrounding the early Republic and its restoration following the Gallic disaster.

1 (**i).   Et qui se sperat Romae regnare Quadratae?

2 (**v).   Septingenti sunt, paulo plus aut minus, anni
                  Augusto augurio postquam incluta condita Roma est

Book 5

Events covered in this book include the execution of the Younger Manlius
in 340 BCE and the battles surrounding Rome's Italic neighbors.

1 (**i).   Moribus antiquis res stat Romana virisque

2 (***ii).   Cives Romani tunc facti sunt Campani

Book 6

This book covers events surrounding the war against King Pyrrhus.

1 (i).   Quis potis ingentis oras evolvere belli

2 (ii).   Navos repertus homo, Graio patre, Graius homo, rex

3 (†iii).   Nomine Burrus uti memorant a stirpe supremo

4 (**iv).   Aio te Aeacidae Romanos vincere posse

5 (**vii).   Proletarius publicitus scutisque feroque
                  ornatur ferro. muros urbemque forumque
                  excubiis curant

6 (ix).   Incedunt arbusta per alta, securibus caedunt,
                  percellent magnas quercus, exciditur ilex,
                  fraxinus frangitur atque abies consternitur alta,
                  pinus proceras pervertunt: omne sonabat
                  arbustum fremitu silvai frondosai.

7 (**xi).   Nec mi aurum posco, nec mi pretium dederitis;
                  nec cauponantes bellum, sed belligerentes
                  ferro non auro vitam cernamus utrique:
                  vosne velit an me regnare era, quidve ferat Fors,
                  virtute experiamur. Et hoc simul accipe dictum;
                  quorum virtuti belli fortuna pepercit,
                  eorundem libertati me parcere certum est.
                  Dono, ducite, doque volentibus cum magnis dis.

Book 7

Book 7 covers events from the First Punic War to the Second Punic
War.

1(**i).   scripsere alii rem
                  vorsibus quos olim Faunei vatesque canebant

2 (**ia).   [cum] neque Musarum scopulos [...]
nec dicti studiosus [quisquam erat] ante hunc
Nos ausi reserare [...]

3 (ii).   Nec quisquam sophiam, sapientia quae perhibetur,
in somnis vidit prius quam sam discere coepit

4 (**iv).   Poeni soliti suos sacrificare puellos

5 (***vi).   Appius indixit Carthaginiensibus bellum

6 (*x).   Corpore tartarino prognata Paluda virago
cui par imber et ignis, spiritus et gravis terra

7 (xi).   Sulpureas posuit spiramina Naris ad undas

8 (xii).   longique cupressi
stant rectis foliis et amaro corpore buxum

9 (**xiii).   postquam Discordia taetra
belli ferratos postes portasque refregit

10 (***xv).   Marsa manus, Paeligna cohors, Vestina virum vis

11 (xix).   Fortibus est fortuna viris data

12 (xxi).   Denique vi magna quadrupes, eques atque elephanti
proiciunt sese

13 (**xxiv).   Iuno Vesta Minerva Ceres Diana Venus Mars
Mercurius Iovis Neptunus Volcanus Apollo

Book 8

Book 8 narrates events surrounding the Hannibalic War.

1 (iv).   Multa dies in bello conficit unus

              Et rursus multae fortunae forte recumbunt:
haud quaquam quemquam semper fortuna secuta est

2 (vii).   Consequitur. Summo sonitu quatit ungula terram

3 (†xii).   Haece locutus vocat quocum bene saepe libenter
mensam sermonesque suos rerumque suarum
consilium partit, magnam quom lassus diei
partem trivisset de summis rebus regundis,
consilio indu foro lato sanctoque senatu;
quoi res audacter magnas parvasque iocumque
eloqueretur †et cuncta† malaque et bona dictu
evomeret si qui vellet tutoque locaret;
quocum multa volup

gaudia clamque palamque,
ingenium quoi nulla malum sententia suadet
ut faceret facinus levis aut malus; doctus, fidelis,
suavis homo, iucundus, suo contentus, beatus,
scitus, secunda loquens in tempore, commodus, verbum
paucum, multa tenens antiqua, sepulta vetustas
quae facit, et mores veteresque novosque, †tenentem
multorum veterum leges divomque hominumque,
prudentem qui dicta loquive tacereve posset:
Hunc inter pugnas conpellat Serilius sic.

4 (**xv).   [Serv. *ad Aen. 1.20: (in Ennio inducitur)*
                 Iuppiter promittens Romanis excidium Carthaginis]

5 (**xvi).   [Serv. *ad Aen. 1.281: bello Punico secundo, ut ait*
                 Ennius, placata Iuno coepit favere Romanis]

Book 9

A continuing account of events surrounding the Hannibalic War.

1 (vi).   Additur orator Cornelius suaviloquenti
                 ore Cethegus Marcus Tuditano collega
                 Marci filius. Is dictus popularibus ollis
                 qui tum vivebant homines atque aevom agitabant
                 flos delibatus populi Suadaique medulla.

Book 10

The narrative of the Macedonian War begins with a short proem.

1 (**i).   Insece Musa manu Romanorum induperator
                 quod quisque in bello gessit cum rege Philippo

Book 11

The fragments from this book cannot be placed in secure contexts, but
they seem to describe the Roman victory over Philip and the declaration
of freedom for Greece at the Isthmian Games in 196 BCE.

Book 12

The two main events treated in this book seem to be the campaign against
Nabis of Sparta and the victories in Spain (195 BCE), of Ennius' former
patron, Cato.

1 (i).   Unus homo nobis cunctando restituit rem.
                 Noenum rumores ponebat ante salutem.
                 Ergo postque magisque viri nunc gloria claret.

2 (ii).   Omnes mortales victores, cordibus vivis
                 laetantes, vino curatos somnus repente
                 in campo passim mollissimus perculit acris

Book 13

Outbreak of the Syrian War.

1 (**i).   Isque Hellesponto pontem contendit in alto

2 (iii).   Hannibal audaci cum pectore de me hortatur
                 ne bellum faciam, quem credidit esse meum cor
                 suasorem summum et studiosum robore belli

3 (iv).   satin vates verant aetate in agunda

Book 14

Various battles are described.

1 (ii).   Labitur uncta carina, volat super impetus undas.

2 (iii).   Verrunt extemplo placidum mare: marmore flavo
                 caeruleum spumat sale conferta rate pulsum

3 (iv).   Quom procul aspiciunt hostes accedere ventis
                 navibus velivolis

4 (vii).   Horrescit telis exercitus asper utrimque

5 (ix).   Omnes occisi occensique in nocte serena

Book 15

Description of Nobilior's Aetolian campaign and the seige of Ambracia.

1 (**i).   [Aur. Vict. *vir. ill. 52: M. Fulvius Nobilior ... consul
                 Aetolos ... proeliis frequentibus victos et in Ambraciam
                 oppidum coactos in deditionem accepit ... de quibus tri-
                 umphavit: quam victoriam per se magnificam Q. Ennius
                 amicus eius insigni laude celebravit.]*

2 (v).   Undique conveniunt velut imber tela tribuno:
                 configunt parmam, tinnit hastilibus umbo,
                 aerato sonitu galeae, sed nec pote quisquam
                 undique nitendo corpus discerpere ferro.
                 Semper abundantes hastas frangitque quatitque.
                 Totum sudor habet corpus, multumque laborat,
                 nec respirandi fit copia: praepete ferro
                 Histri tela manu iacientes sollicitabant.

Book 16

In a proem, Ennius describes his return to the composition of the Annales in his old age.

1 (i).	post aetate pigret sufferre laborem
2 (ii).	hebem
3 (iii).	Quippe vetusta virum non est satis bella moveri
4 (iv).	Reges per regnum statuasque sepulcraque quaerunt, aedificant nomen, summa nituntur opum vi
5 (v).	Postremo longinqua dies confecerit aetas
6 (vi).	[Pliny, *H.N. 7.101: Q. Ennius T. Caecilium Teucrum fratremque eius praecipue miratus propter eos sextum decimum adiecit annalem.*]

Book 17

The surviving fragments of Book 17 cannot be connected with a specific event.

1 (v).	Concurrunt veluti venti, quom spiritus Austri imbricitor Aquiloque suo cum flamine contra indu mari magno fluctus extollere certant

Book 18

The two surviving fragments from this book cannot be placed in any thematic context.

Sedis Incertae Fragmenta

1 (***xi).	Musas quas memorant nosce esse Camenas
2 (**lxix).	Sicuti fortis equos spatio qui saepe supremo Vicit Olympia nunc senio confectus quiescit
3 (lxx).	[Aul. Gell. N.A. 17.21.43: *Claudium et Tuditanem consules sequuntur C. Valerius et C. Mamilius, quibus natum esse Q. Ennium poetam M. Varro in primo de poetis libro scripsit, eumque cum septimum et sexagesimum annum ageret duodecimum* (XXII eraso X priore X) *annalem scripsisse idque ipsum Ennium in eodem libro dicere.*]
4 (**lxxii).	Nos sumus Romani qui fuimus ante Rudini

VI. COMEDY

Caecilius Statius

Plocium

This play is based on the *Plokion* of Menander (fragments of both plays compared by Aulus Gellius *N.A.* 2.23.11), in which a girl was raped by her future fiancé (neither knew the identity of the other). Pregnancy was detected by the girl's family slave, Parmeno. When the fiancé discovered that his intended bride was pregnant, the wedding was called off. The bride's family went to court and, based on the evidence of a necklace (*plocium*) which the fiancé/rapist recognized, the estranged couple was married.

The fiancé's father (F), after a monologue, converses with a neighbour (N) about troublesome wives:

1.   (F) Is demum miser est qui aerumnam suam nesciat occultare
      foris: ita me uxor forma et factis facit, si taceam, tamen indicium,
      quae nisi dotem omnia quae nolis habet: qui sapiet de me discet,
      qui quasi ad hostis captus liber servio salva urbe atque arce.
      Dum eius mortem inhio, egomet inter vivos vivo mortuus.
      Quaen mihi quidquid placet eo privatum it me servatam <velim>?
      Ea me clam se cum mea ancilla ait consuetum; id me arguit:
      ita plorando orando instando atque obiurgando me optudit,
            eam uti venderem. Nunc credo inter suas
            aequalis, cognatas sermonem serit:
                  'Quis vostrarum fuit integra aetatula
                        quae hoc idem a viro
                  impetrarit suo, quod ego anus modo
            effeci, paelice ut meum privarem virum?'
      Haec erunt concilia hocedie: differar sermone misere.[23]

---

23 Text and fragment numbers are from Otto Ribbeck, (*CRF*), 68-77. I have added
conjectures for the speakers to Ribbeck's text.

2. (N) Sed tua morosane uxor quaeso est? (F) Va! Rogas?
    (N) Qui tandem? (F) Taedet mentionis quae, mihi
    ubi domum adveni, adsedi, extemplo savium
    dat ieiuna anima. (F) Nil peccat de savio;
    ut devomas vult quod foris potaveris.

3. Placere occepit graviter, postquam emortuast.

4. (Parmeno):
    Soletne mulier decimo mense parere? – Pol nono quoque,

    etiam septimo atque octavo.

5. (Parmeno):
    Pudebat, credo, commemoramentum stupri.

6. (Girl's father?):
    Properatim in tenebris istuc confectum est opus.

7. (?)
    Consequitur comes insomnia, ea porro insaniam affert.

8. (Parmeno):
         ... is demum infortunatust homo,
    pauper qui educit in egestatem liberos;
    cui fortuna et res nuda est, continuo patet.
    Nam opulento famam facile occultat factio.

9. (Girl's father?):
    Edepol, senectus, si nil quicquam aliud viti
    adportes tecum, cum advenis, unum id sat est,
    quod diu vivendo multa quae non volt videt.

10. (?)
    Patiere quod dant, quando optata non danunt.

11. (?)
    Vivas ut possis, quando nec quis ut velis.

12. (?)
    Abi intro atque istaec aufer; tamen hodie extollat nuptias.

13. (?)
    Quid hoc futurum obsoniost ubi tantum sumpti factum?

14. Insanum auspicium: <haut> aliter histrionium est,
    atque ut magistratus, publicae <rei> cum auspicant

15. (?)
    Tu nurum non vis odiosam tibi esse, quam rarenter videas?

16. (Girl's father?):
    Ibo ad forum et pauperii tutelam geram.

17. (Girl's father):
    Ibo domum: ad plebem pergitur: publicitus defendendumst.

18. (Fiancé's mother Crobyle?):
    opulentitate nostra sibi <esse> iniuriam
    factam.

19. (? To Parmeno):
    Liberne es? (Parmeno): Non sum, verum inibi est ...

20. catellae

VII. TRAGEDY II

Pacuvius

Antiopa

The Greek model for the *Antiopa* was Euripides' play of the same name. The myth of Antiopa revolves around her rape by Zeus, after which she fled from her father Nycteus, King of Boeotia, to Sicyon where she married Epopeus. Upon Nycteus' death, his brother Lycus and his wife Dirce punished Antiopa by killing Epopeus and imprisoning her. At some point in her journey Antiopa gave birth to twins, Amphion and Zethus, whom she exposed, but they were raised by shepherds. It was while fleeing prison that Antiopa was accidentally reunited with her sons, who helped her punish Lycus and Dirce for their crimes. In Pacuvius' play, Amphion and Zethus are adult herdsmen who bide their time in sophistic debate until the chance arrival of their hitherto unknown mother, Antiopa. Upon discovering her identity, the twins punish Dirce who has attempted to recapture her.[24] Since Dirce is punished and Antiopa is reunited with her sons, is the play properly a comedy?

The surviving fragments are somewhat difficult to place within the dramatic action of the play. The most problematic fragments are the lines in which Antiopa reveals her identity to the twins, since it is unclear whether they appear before or after Dirce's arrival on stage.

Fragment 1 informs the audience of the twins' identity:

1.   Iovis ex Antiopa Nyctei nati <duo>[25]

---

24 In Propertius' version of the myth (3.15), Antiopa escapes from Dirce and dis-
    covers her sons, but finds Amphion the more sympathetic of the two. The later
    rivalry between the sons during the construction of the walls of Thebes is also
    described.

25 Quoted are the text and fragment numbers from Ribbeck (*TRF*), 86-90.

2. [Rhet. *ad Herenn.* 22.27,43: *item verendum est, ne de alia re dicatur, cum alia de re controversia sit... uti apud Pacuvium Zethus cum Amphione, quorum controversia de musica inducta est, disputatio in sapientiae rationem et virtutis utilitatem consumitur.*]

A playful insult from one twin to the other:

3. Loca horrida initas.[26]

In fragment 4, Amphion poses a riddle to the chorus of city dwellers (*Astici*), who were perhaps present in this scene as judges to the debate between Amphion and Zethus:

4. Amphio:
    Quadrupes tardigrada agrestis humilis aspera,
    Brevi capite, cervice anguina, aspectu truci,
    Eviscerata inanima cum animali sono.

    Astici:
    Ita saeptuosa dictione abs te datur
    Quod coniectura sapiens aegre contuit:
    Non intellegimus, nisi si aperte dixeris.

    Amphio:
    Testudo.[27]

Fragments 5-7 come from Antiopa's speech, or series of speeches, in which she relates the punishment she has endured from Lycus and Dirce. One cannot assume, however, that these lines immediately preceded the revelation of her identity at this point in the play.

5. ...perdita inluvie atque insomnia

6. Frendere noctes, misera quas perpessa sum

7. ...fruges frendo sola saxi robore.

The context and placement of fragment 8 is unclear:

8.   ...sol si perpetuo siet,
    Flammeo vapore torrens terrae fetum exusserit:
    Nocti ni interveniat, fructus per pruinam obriguerint.

---

26 Warmington, (*ROL* II), 160-161, ascribes this line to Amphion, together with the following line which Ribbeck ascribes to unassigned fragments:
    Tu cornifrontes pascere armentas soles.

27 Following this fragment, Warmington, (*ROL* II), 164-165, gives the following line to Zethus: *Odi ego homines ignava opera et philosopha sententia.*

Fragment 9 seems to be a speech by Antiopa, but the addressee is unknown:

9.   Minitabiliterque increpare dictis saevis incipit.

In Fragment 10, Zethus (?) orders Antiopa away from the animal pens:

10.   Nonne hinc vos propere <e> stabulis amolimini?

Fragment 11 seems to come from a speech by the shepherd who discovered the twins as infants on Mount Cithaeron:

11.   Sed cum animo attendi ad quaerendum, quid siet?

Dirce arrives on stage with a second chorus of Maenads in pursuit of Antiopa in fragment 12:

12.   ....cervicum
Floros dispendite crines.[28]

Antiopa addresses her sons in fragment 13, but whether or not her identity had been revealed before this point is unclear:

13.   Salvete, gemini, mea propages sanguinis!

14.   [Persius I, 77: *sunt quos Pacuviusque et verrucosa moretur Antiopa, aerumnis cor luctificabile fulta.*]

In fragment 15, Antiopa describes the filthy state in which she was kept as Dirce's captive:

15.   ....inluvie corporis
Et coma prolixa impexa conglomerata atque horrida.

16.   [Martianus *Capella* III 257: *nam Setum dicebant quem nunc Zethum dicunt.*]

It is not clear whether the punishment of Dirce occured off-stage and was reported by a messenger or whether it was simply alluded to following the reconciliation scene.

---

28 Warmington,(*ROL* II), 166-167 (= Ribbeck (*TRF*), Pacuvius: *Ex Incertis Fabulis,* 4), adds the following fragment found in the unassigned fragments of Pacuvius after fragment 11, but it may actually belong to Dirce's entrance speech as she plots further punishment for Antiopa:

      Agite ite evolvite rapite, coma
      tractate per aspera saxa et humum;
      scindite vestem ocius!

Teucer

The model for Pacuvius' *Teucer* was Sophocles' play of the same name, but it is Sophocles' *Ajax* which provides information to otherwise confusing details about his myth. Teucer was the son of Telamon and Hesione and the half-brother of Ajax. Throughout the *Iliad*, Teucer protected his half-brother Ajax in battle against the Trojans. Following the Trojan War, Teucer was absent when Ajax committed suicide following his rivalry with Odysseus over Achilles' weapons. At some later time, he gave proper burial to the remains of Ajax. The son of Ajax, Eurysaces, also died at this time. Upon Teucer's return to Salamis, Telamon blamed him for not protecting Ajax and refused to receive him home, so the plot centers around Teucer's recognition and rejection. Teucer then founded a colony on Cyprus, called Salamis.

The play deals with events following Teucer's return to Salamis. A relatively high number of fragments from the play survive, but the exact placement of the fragments within the dramatic action of the play remains unclear.

Fragment 1 describes the wasted appearance of a woman, who may be Hesione:

1.   Quae desiderio alumnum, paenitudine,
      squale scabreque, inculta vastitudine [29]

Fragment 2 describes Telamon's anxiety concerning the return of his sons, indicating that he has not yet learned of Ajax' suicide:

2.   Post quam defessus perrogitandod advenas
      \<fuit\> de gnatis, neque quemquam invenit scium

3.   Neque perpetrare precibus inpetrita quit.

The identity of the recently arrived Teucer is unknown:

4.   Nihilne a Troia adportat fando? ...
      Teucer's identity is discovered in fragment 5?

5.   Quam te post multis tueor tempestatibus!

The following fragment deals with the disastrous *nostoi* of the Greeks:

6.   Periere Danai, plera pars pessum datast.

The following fragments concern the death of Ajax:

7.   Profusus gemitu, murmure 'occisti' antruat.

---

29 Quoted are the text and fragment numbers from Ribbeck (*TRF*), 134-139.

8.   Nos illum interea proliciendo propitiaturos facul
      remur.

9.   nam Teucrum regi sapsa res restibiliet.

Telamon speaks:

10.   Haud sinam quidquam profari prius quam accepso quod peto.

Telamon wishes to speak to Teucer alone:

11.   Facessite omnes hinc: parumper tu mane!

Telamon chides Teucer:

12.   Segregare abs te ausu's aut sine illo Salaminam ingredi,
      neque paternum aspectum es veritus, quom aetate exacta indigem
      liberum lacerasti orbasti exstinxti, neque fratris necis
      neque eius gnati parui, qui tibi in tutelam est traditus...?

Teucer describes his voyage home to Telamon:

13.   mihi classem imperat
      Thessalum nostramque in altum ut properiter deducerem.

14.   Rapide retro citroque percito aestu praecipitem ratem
      reciprocare, undaeque e gremiis subiectare adfligere.

15.   ... armamentum stridor, flictus navium,
      strepitus fremitus, clamor tonitruum et rudentum sibilus

16.   ubi poetae pro suad arte falsa confictan autumant,
      qui causam humilem dictis amplent

Telamon's rage endures:

17.   Quamquam annisque et aetate hoc corpus putret.

Teucer speaks?

18.   Aut me occide, illinc si usquam probitam gradum.

Telamon speaks:

19.   Te repudio nec recipio: naturam abdico: i facesse!

20.   ...ut ego, si quisquam me tagit

21.   nisi coerceo
      protervitatem atque hostio ferociam.

Ex Incertis Fabulis

44. Nerei repandirostrum incurvicervicum pecus.[30]

45. ... profectione laeti piscium lasciviam
      intuetur, nec tuendi satietas capier potest.
      Interea prope iam occidente sole inhorrescit mare,
      tenebrae conduplicantur, noctisque et nimbum obcaecat nigror,
      flamma inter nubes coruscat, caelum tonitur contremit,
      grando mixta imbri largifico subita precipitans cadit,
      undique omnes venti erumpunt, saevi existunt turbines,
      fervit aestu pelagus. [31]

50. flexanima tamquam lymphata aut Bacchi sacris
      commota, in tumulis Teucrum commemorans suum[32]

Accius

Medea sive Argonautae

The surviving fragments of the *Medea sive Argonautae* bear a remark-
able resemblance to the story found in Apollonius Rhodes, *Argonautica* IV,
303 ff, in which Medea murders her brother Apsyrtus, who was leading an
expedition of Colchians against the Argonauts. Some have conjectured a
play by Sophocles as the possible model, but the play's fragments, revealing
that Apsyrtus was a boy, suggest the version of the myth in which Medea
kidnaps her brother and throws pieces of his cut-up corpse to delay the
Colchian fleet.[33] One cannot rule out that this was an original composition
in which Accius dramatized a story found in Greek epic, since he appears
to have based two of his plays, the *Epinausimache* and *Nyctegressia*, upon
episodes in Homer's *Iliad*.

---

30 Ribbeck,(*TRF*),152-153: *"Vix dubium quin ad Teucrum pertineant."*
31 This fragment is cited by Cicero, *de Div.*, I, 14, 24, but the play is not specified.
    Cicero does introduce the fragment, however, by stating that the Greeks, despite
    being joyous at the prospect of returning home from Troy, nevertheless were
    dependent on the fallible pilots of their ships. Ribbeck (*TRF*), 153, does not
    assign this passage to the *Teucer*, but notes that similar descriptions are found
    in the play: *"Naufragium in Teucro enarratum est: cf. XIV et XV."*
32 Ribbeck, (*TRF*),154: *"Non dubium quin de Hesiona haec in Teucro narrata
    fuerint."*
33 Warmington, (*ROL* II), 456, following Ribbeck (*RT*),528-536, suggests a play
    by Sophocles as the possible model, but the closest play of Sophocles on the
    Medea myth is the *Scythians,* in which Apsyrtus appears as a boy. See Hugh
    Lloyd Jones, *Sophocles III, Fragments* Loeb Classical Library (Cambridge, MA,
    and London, 1996) 274-277.

The play covers events following the Argonauts' theft of the golden fleece. After Jason and Medea flee Colchis with the Argonauts, they land briefly at the mouth of the Ister River to discuss a plan of attack against Medea's brother Apsyrtus, who was pursuing them with a fleet of Colchians. They resolve that Medea, under false pretenses, should request a meeting with her brother in order to murder him.

The play opens with the arrival of the Argo, which terrifies the barbarian shepherd(s) who has never seen a ship before:

1.   Tanta moles labitur
        fremibunda ex alto ingenti sonitu et spiritu;
        prae se undas volvit, vortices vi suscitat:
        ruit prolapsa, pelagus respargit reflat.
        Ita dum interruptum credas nimbum volvier,
        dum quod sublime ventis expulsum rapi
        saxum aut procellis, vel globosos turbines
        existere ictos undis concursantibus:
        nisi quas terrestris pontus strages conciet,
        aut forte Triton fuscina evertens specus
        supter radices penitus undante in freto
        molem ex profundo saxeam ad caelum erigit. [34]

2/3.   sicut lascivi atque alacres rostris perfremunt
        delphini, item alto mulcta Silvani melo
        consimilem ad auris cantum et auditum refert.

4.   Ego me extollo in abietem, alte ex tuto prospectum aucupo.

5.   apud vetustam turrem

6.   Vagant, pavore pecuda in tumulis deserunt.
        <A!> qui vos pascet postea?

In fragments 7 and 8, Jason seems to explain the ship and the various stages of civilization to the shepherd(s):

7.   Prima ex immani victum ad mansuetum applicans.

8.   ut tristis turbinum
        toleraret hiemes, mare cum horreret fluctibus.

In fragment 9, Medea discusses how she will lure Apsyrtus under false pretenses.

9.   Nisi ut astu ingenium lingua laudem et dictis lactem lenibus.

In fragments 10-11, Medea seems to assure Jason that she is capable of effecting supernatural results.

---

34 Quoted are the text and fragment numbers of Ribbeck, (TRF), 216-220.

10.   Exul inter hostes exspes expers desertus vagus.

11.   perite in stabulo frenos inmittens feris.

In line 12, an unknown speaker addresses Medea:

12.   Tun dia Mede's, cuius aditum expectans pervixi usque adhuc?

Is Jason the speaker of fragments 13-14, based on *Argonautica* 395 ff., where he calms Medea's fears of being abandoned by him?

13.   Qui potis est refelli quisquam ubi nullust causandi locus?

14.   Principio extispicium ex prodigiis congruens ars te arguit.

After the murder of Apsyrtus and the flight of Jason and Medea, Aeetes laments the death of his son. Aeetes' presence in the play is surprising, since nowhere in Apollonius' version does Aeetes pursue the Argonauts.

15.   Lavere salsis vultum lacrumis...

16.   Pernici orbificor liberorum leto et tabificabili.

In fragment 17, the chorus or Aeetes laments the unpredictablility of life?

17.   Fors dominatur, neque quicquam ulli
       proprium in vita est.

Ex Incertis Incertorum Fabulis

93.   posquam pater
       adpropinquat iamque paene ut comprehendatur parat,
       puerum interea optruncat membraque articulatim dividit,
       perque agros passim dispergit corpus: id ea gratia,
       ut, dum nati dissupatos artus captaret parens,
       ipsa interea effugeret, illum ut maeror tarderet sequi,
       sibi salutem ut familiari pareret parricidio.[35]

Philocteta sive Philocteta Lemnius

The Greek model (or models) for the *Philocteta sive Philocteta Lemnius* is unknown.[36] The events of the play fall outside of the *Iliad's* narrative. In Sophocles' version, Odysseus and Neoptolemus open the play, and the

---

35 Ribbeck conjectures that this fragment belongs to this play: "*Adiungendum praeterea inc. inc. fab. XCIII videtur.*"

36 Ribbeck (*RT*), 376-381, argues that the play is a combination of plays by Aeschylus, Sophocles, and Euripides. Warmington, (*ROL* II), 504-505, suggests that at least part of the play is based on a play by Aeschylus.

chorus consists of sailors, not Lemnians as in Accius' version. The plot
of the play is recoverable due to the numerous fragments which survive.
While the Greeks were sailing to Troy, Philoctetes was bitten in the ankle
by a snake and abandoned on the island of Lemnos in possession of arrows
which had once belonged to Hercules. Later, Agamemnon ordered Ulysses
and Diomedes to retrieve the arrows when he learned Troy would not fall
without them. Philoctetes was brought to Troy, where his foot was cured
by Machaon.

The play opens with fragments 1 and 2, which are spoken by the chorus
and addressed to Ulysses.

1.   Inclute, parva prodite patria,
       nomine celebri claroque potens
       pectore, Achivis classibus ductor,
       gravis Dardaniis gentibus ultor,
       Laertidae![37]

2.   Lemnia praesto
       litora rara, et celsa Cabirum
       delubra tenes, misteria quae
       pristina castis concepta sacris
       [...]
       Volcania <iam> templa sub ipsis
       collibus, in quos delatus locos
       dicitur alto ab limine caeli
       [...]
       nemus expirante vapore vides,
       unde ignis cluet mortalibus clam
       divusus: eum dictus Prometheus
       clepsisse dolo poenasque Iovi
       fato expendisse supremo.

In fragment 3, Ulysses inquires after Philoctetes:

3.   ...ubi habet? urbe agrone? ...

A shepherd (?) describes Philoctetes' wound:

4.   Quem neque tueri contra nec adfari queas.

5.   Configit tardus celeris, stans volatilis,
       [..]
       pro veste pinnis membra textis contegit.

In fragment 6, Ulysses plans his approach to Philoctetes:

---

37 Quoted are the text and fragment numbers of Ribbeck (*TRF*), 236-242.

6.   Contra est eundum cautim et captandum mihi.

Philoctetes expresses his anger against the Greeks and his obscure location, far from the other inhabitants of the island:

7.   ... cui potestas si deter, tua
      cupienter malis membra discerpat suis.

8.   caprigenum trita ungulis.

In fragments 9-12, Philoctetes complains of his festering wound:

9.   Reciproca tendens nervo equino concita
      tela

10.   ... pinnigero, non armigero in corpore
      tela exercentur haec abiecta gloria.

11.   <iaceo> in tecto umido
      quod eiulatu questu gemitu fremitibus
      resonando mutum flebilis voces refert.

12.   E viperino morsu venae viscerum
      veneno inbutae taetros cruciatus cient.

Philoctetes, seeing Ulysses (and Diomedes?), addresses him in fragments 13-15, but it is not clear exactly when Ulysses reveals his identity:

13.   Quis tu es mortalis, qui in deserta et tesqua te adportes loca?

14.   quod te obsecro, aspernabilem
      Nec haec taetritudo mea me inculta faxsit...

15.   Contempla hanc sedem, in qua ego novem hiemes saxo stratus
      pertuli.

16.   heu Mulciber!
      Arma <ergo> ignavo invicta es fabricatus manu.

17.   Ipsam Frygiam mitiorem esse <aio> immani Graecia.

Philoctetes speaks:

18.   Pari dyspari, si inpar esses tibi, ego nunc non essem miser.

Philoctetes complains of his pain:

19.   Heu! quis salsis fluctibus mandet
      me ex sublimo vertice saxi?
      Iam iam absumor: conficit animam
            Vis vulneris, ulceris aestus.

20.   Sub axe posita ad stellas septem, unde horrifer
      Aquilonis stridor gelidas molitur nives.

In a part of the play now missing, Ulysses convinces Philoctetes to ac-
company the embassy back to Troy, since in fragment 21, Philoctetes
prepares to leave Lemnos:

21.   Agite ac vulnus ne succusset gressus, caute ingredimini.

The context of the final fragment is unclear but may belong with the
fragments describing Philoctetes' wound:

22.   dracontem

The play ends with the reconciliation between Philoctetes and Odysseus
and the fated victory of the Greeks in the Trojan War, so it seems more
properly a comedy than a tragedy.

VIII. Satire

Lucilius

Satires

(Selections)

Book 1

Book 1 contains a Council of the gods:

1.   Consilium summis hominum de rebus habebant.[38]
     (Marx, 2)

Jupiter speaks:

2.   quo populum atque urbem pacto servare potisset
     amplius Romanam.
     (Marx, 5)

Apollo speaks:

3.   'ut
     nemo sit nostrum quin aut pater optimus divum,
     aut Neptunus pater, Liber Saturnus pater, Mars
     Ianus Quirinus pater siet ac dicatur ad unum ...
     (Marx, 20-22)

4.   Lupus princeps senatus fuit.
     (Marx, 47*)

Book 2

Book 2 contains a description of the trial of Q. Mucius Scaevola (cos. 117 BCE), who was accused of administrative improprities, by Albucius, while he was governor of Asia.

---

38 Text of F. Marx, 1-95, with his fragment numbers in parentheses.

Book 3

Book 3 describes an *iter Siculum:*

1. Praeterea omne iter est hoc labosum atque lutosum.
    (Marx, 109)

2. verum haec ludus ibi, susque omnia deque fuerunt,
    susque et deque fuere, inquam, omnia ludus iocusque:
    illud opus durum, ut Setinum accessimus finem,
    aigilipes montes, Aenae omnes, asperi Athones.
    (Marx, 110-113)

3. Hinc media remis Palinurus pervenio nox.
    (Marx, 127)

4. Caupona hic tamen una Syra...
    (Marx, 128)

Book 4

Book 4 contains a description of a gladiatorial combat between Aeserninus
the Samnite and Pacideianus.

1. Aeserninus fuit Flaccorum mune<re> quidam
    Samnis, spurcus homo, vita illa dignu locoque.
    Cum Pacideiano conponitur, optimus multo
    post homines natos gladiator qui fuit unus.
    (Marx, 149-152)

Pacideianus speaks:

2. 'Occidam illum equidem et vincam, si id quaeritis,' inquit,
    'verum illud credo fore: in os prius occipiam ipse,
    quam gladium in stomacho furia ac pulmonibus sisto:
    odi hominem, iratus pugno, nec longius quicquam
    nobis, quam dextrae gladium dum accommodet alter;
    usque adeo, studio atque odio illius, ecferor ira.'

Book 5

In Book 5, Lucilius writes a letter to a friend who did not visit him when
he was ill.

1. Quo me habeam pacto, tam etsi non quaeris, docebo,
    quando in eo numero mansi quo in maxima non est
    pars hominum...
    ut per<i>sse velis, quem visere nolueris, cum
    debueris. Hoc 'nolueris' et 'debueris' te
    si minus delectat (quod atechnon) et Eissocratium hoc

lerodesque simul totum ac si miraciodes,
non operam perdo, si tu hic.
(Marx, 181-188)

Book 6

Scipio Aemilianus meets a bore:

1.   Cui neque iumentum est nec servus nec comes ullus:
bulgam, et quidquid habet nummorum, secum habet ipse,
cum bulga cenat, dormit, lavit. Omnia in una
sunt homini bulga: bulga haec devincta <la>certo est.
(243-246)

Book 7

Book 7 seems to contain satirical scenes about sex:

1.   Hanc ubi vult male habere, ulcisci pro scelere eius,
testam sumit homo Samiam sibi, 'anu noceo' inquit,
praecidit caulem testisque una amputat ambo.

Dixi. ad principium venio. Vetulam atque virosam
uxorem caedam potius quam castrem egomet me.
(279-283)

Book 8

This book also contains sexual material, but the fragments are too few to reconstruct descriptions with any certainty.

Book 9

This book contains Lucilius' theories on lexography and definitions of literary terms:

1.   Non haec quid valeat, quidve hoc intersiet illud,
cognoscis. Primum hoc, quod dicimus esse poema.
Pars est parva poema <poesis>.
(Marx, *Satire 2, 338-340*)

Book 10

A literary dispute between Lucilius and Accius?

1.   [Porphyrio *ad Horatii serm. I.10,53: 'Nil comis tragici mutat Lucilius Acci?' "Facit autem haec Lucilius cum alias tum vel maxime in tertio libro: meminit VIIII et X."*]

Books 11-14

Book 11 contains character sketches of prominent Romans, but the frag-
ments from Books 12 –14 are too few to determine the themes of the
satires they contained.

Book 15

Book 15 considers philosophical and religious (superstitious) questions:

1.   Multa homines portenta in Homeri versibus ficta
      Monstra putant, quorum in primis Polyphemus ducentos
      Cyclops longus pedes: et porro huic maius bacillum
      Quam malus navi e corbita maximus ullast.
      (Marx, 480-483)

2.   Terriculas, Lamias, Fauni quas Pompiliique
      instituere Numae, tremit has, hic omnia ponit.
      Ut pueri infantes credunt signa omnia aena
      vivere et esse homines, sic isti somnia ficta
      vera putant, credunt signis cor inesse in aenis.
      Pergula fictorum veri nihil, omnia ficta.
      (Marx, 484-489)

Book 16

1.   [Porphyrio, *ad Hor. Carm 1.22.10: 'dum meam canto Lalagen.'* Id
      est carmen in Lalagen nomine amicam compositum sicut scilicet
      Liber Lucilii XVI Collyra inscribitur eo quod de Collyra amica
      scriptus sit.]

Books 17-19

The context of these books is unclear from the few surviving fragments.

Book 20

Book 20 describes a banquet given by Q. Granius (*trib. pleb.*) (L. Licin-
ius Crassus' auctioneer) in 107 BCE which includes a description of a
shipwreck.

Book 21

No fragments survive.

Books 22-25

In these books, Lucilius seems to describe his freedmen and slaves in
elegiac couplets.

Book 26

As the former first book of Lucilius' collection, Book 26 defines the nature of his poetry. Fragments are mostly in Saturnians, with hexameter verse first appearing in Book 30.

1. Persium non curo legere, Laelium Decumum volo.
    (Marx, 593*)

2. Lucilius or interlocutor describes dangers of attacking contemporaries, as Naevius did?:

    hic cruciatur fame,
    frigore, inluvie, inbalnitie, inperfunditie, incuria
    (Marx, 509-600)

3. quid cavendum tibi censerem, quid vitandum maxume.
    (Marx, 609)

4. An interlocutor urges Lucilius to write panegyrics:

    hunc laborem sumas, laudem qui tibi ac fructum ferat:
    percrepa pugnam Popili, facta Corneli cane.
    (Marx, 620-621)

5. Lucilius' vulgar reply:

    ego si, qui sum et quo folliculo nunc sum indutus, non queo,
    ita uti quisque nostrum e bulga est matris in lucem editus...
    (Marx, 622-623)

Book 27

Various subjects include love and the vicissitudes of life:

1. te, Popli, populi salute fictis versibus Lucilius,
    quibus potest inpertit, totumque hoc studiose et sedulo.
    (Marx, 689-690)

Books 28

Book 28 seems to contain three satires in various meters, but only the contexts of two are recoverable: a philosophical discourse set in Athens, and the circumstances surrounding the attack and lawsuit of a Roman citizen.

Book 29

Book 29 contains five satires in various meters. Themes include behavior towards women (in sexual contexts), criticism of tragedy and comedy, and the activities of men in Rome.

1.   amicos hodie cum improbo illo audivimus
   Lucilio advocasse
   (Marx, 821-822)

2.   verum tristis contorto aliquo ex Pacuviano exordio
   (Marx, 875)

Book 30

In Book 30 Lucilius established the hexameter as the permanent meter
for his satires, and included four or five satires. Various themes include
a *cena* and a literary dispute with a comic writer.

1.   quantum haurire animus Musarum e fontibus gestit.
   (Marx, 1008)

2.   cui sua conmittunt mortali claustra Camenae
   (Marx, 1028)

3.   nolito tibi me male dicere posse putare.
   (Marx, 1030)

COMMENTARY

Line and fragment numbers appear in bold.

I. ORAL POETRY

Carmina

1. Charm to cure sore feet.
   Note the repetition of *meis pedibus* in lines 1 and 4 which frames the near rhyme of *teneto* and *maneto* in lines 2 and 3.

2. Rhyme at the Meditrinalia (an October fesitival following the vintage). Meditrina was the Goddess of Healing.
   1 Four two syllable words with the repetition of v sounds. Note the effect of placing the contrasting words *novum* and *vetus* next to each other on both lines. The caesura of each line occurs after the second word producing a balanced line.
   2 *medeor* + dative.

3. Rhyme for weather and harvest.
   Vergil adapts the rhyme at *Georgics* 1.101: *hiberno laetissima pulvere farra.*
   1 Two three-syllable words are followed by two two-syllable words, with the caesura occuring after the second word. The first word of each half is the name of a season, followed by a word describing the soil.
   2 There is a series of a three-syllable word followed by a two-syllable word on each side of the caesura.
   camille = vocative case of *camillus*, boy (priest's attendant).

4. Farmer's Prayer at the Lustratio Agri (a purification ritual performed in April).

1 Mars was originally an agricultural god in Italy, and the repetition of his name at line 20 frames the prayer.
precor and *quaeso* have similar meanings.

2 Repetition: *volens* and *propitius* have similar meanings.

3 Tricolon crescendo.

4 *quoius = cuius.* This phrase is echoed in lines 15 and 20.

5 Another tricolon crescendo with words of similar meaning. The caesura occurs after *terram,* separating the second and third cola.

6 The *suovitaurilia* was a sacrifice of swine, sheep, and a bull.

7 *visos* is balanced by *invisos* and provides repetition.

8 More repetition with words of similar meanings.
viduertas, atis, feminine = sterility.

9 Tricolon crescendo with words of similar meaning.

10 Division of cola with two words beginning with the same letter.

11 *siris=sino*; repetition of idea of turning out well.

12 *salva servassis* is a *figura etymologica* (two words of the same root meaning in noun and verb form).

13 *duis = do*; repetition of meaning.

14 Repetition of line 3.

15 Echo of line 4.

16 Tricolon crescendo of words of similar meaning.

17 *lustri faciendi* means the same thing as *lustrandi.*

19 *macte* = vocative, "honoured one"; *lactentibus* = suckling.

20 Echoes of lines 1 and 15.

21 Repetition of line 19 without *immolandis.*

Versus Populares

1. The puns of this verse depend on the proper names Crassus and Carbo. Licinius Crassus (died 91 BCE) prosecuted the father of G. Papirius Carbo. The trial led to the father's suicide which made enemies of his son and Crassus.
   The line is balanced with the near repetition of the same words before and after the caesura following *factus.*

2. Suetonius (*Jul.* 80.3) reports that this verse was inscribed on a statue of Caesar.
   1 Brutus = Lucius Brutus; caesura following *eiecit.*
   2 Caesar is the unexpressed subject of line 2.

3. Proverb.
   1 Pun on the words *rex* and *recte.*
   2 Repetition of *faciet* and *erit but in reverse order.*

4. Suetonius records that this verse was shouted by Caesar's soldiers during his triumph.

1 Pun on the word *subegit* which means to conquer (militarily and sexually), and alludes to Caesar's affair with King Nicomedes.

2 Repetition of the words *triumphat* and *subegit*, but this time the pun is *triumphat,* again alluding to his sexual conquest of Caesar.

II. VERSE EPITAPHS

For a detailed analysis of the tomb of the Scipios and the dating of these inscriptions, see Harriet I. Flower, *Ancestor Masks and Aristocratic Power in Roman Culture* (Oxford, 1996), 166-180, in particular her discussion of R. Wachter's dating of Barbatus' inscription to a date closer to his death and consequently earlier rather than later than the date of his son's inscription as presented here.

1. L. Cornelio Cn. f. Scipio (Great-grandfather of the elder Scipio Africanus).

a) 1 Line 1 of the original epitaph was painted rather than inscribed, as is the rest of the epitaph.

b) 1 *Cornelius* contradicts the spelling *Cornelio* (nominative case) in line 1, of the original inscription.
   Lucius, as the *praenomen,* should appear first, therefore, the rearrangement of Scipio's name is for poetic purposes; the use of *-us* rather than *-os* indicates a date after 200 BCE; caesura after *Lucius.*

2 *Gnaivod = Gnaeus.*
   fortis vir sapiensque evokes Greek ideal of *kalokagathos* referring to the Greek education of the Scipios.

3 Emphasis on beauty (*forma*) indicates a later, Hellenizing addition to the original inscription.
   fuit should be written in the earlier form *fueit.*
   parisuma = parissima.

4 = Line 2 of the original epitaph.
   consol and *censor* should be written in the earlier forms *cosol* and *cesor.*
   quei = qui.

5 The final m is not written for *Taurasia, Cisauna, and Samnio* to indicate that these words are in the accusative case and direct objects of *cepit.* The reason why the final m is not written at times is unclear: the final m appears for *Loucanam* in line 6, which is followed by a vowel, but in epitaph 2, line 5, the final m is missing for *Corsica Aleriaque urbe,* even though all three words are

in the accusative case and *Corsica* is followed by a vowel.
6 *subigit* = *subegit*.
opsides = hostages.

2. L. Cornelio L. f. Scipio:
This epitaph is more recent than the first one (this is the tomb of Barbatus' son), but the archaizing elements evoke the language of an even earlier date. The language, however, is at odds with its innovative poetic style and the result is an epitaph that is at once archaizing and modern.
a) 1-2 These are the oldest lines of the epitaph and are painted rather than inscribed, as is the rest of the epitaph.
b) 1 *Honc* = *hunc*
oino = *unum*. The final m is missing, but is written for *Luciom* in line 3.
ploirume = *plurimi*.
cosentiont = *consentiunt*. The use of *–n* is inconsistent: it is not written here but appears in *consol* and *censor* in line 4.
R[omai] = *Romae*: the locative case.
2 *Duonoro...viro* = *bonorum virorum*.
fuise = *fuisse*.
3 *Luciom Scipione. Filios Barbati*. In the more recent inscription Scipio's name appears in line 3, rather than the more usual position of the deceased's name in line 1, as it is in the original inscription. The placement of the name in line 3 and the period which divides the line into two halves points to a poetic treatment: the scrambled word order of the name (should be *Lucius Barbati filius Scipio*) divides the poem into two approximate halves with the name itself divided into two, making Scipio the subject of each half of the inscription.
filios = *filius*. The spelling out of *filius* rather than the usual abbreviation *–f* emphasizes Barbatus' relation to his father, to mark his own identity.
4 The n's in *consol* and *censor* are more appropriate to Latin of the date of the reworked inscription versus the archaic spelling of these offices in line 2 of the original epitaph.
aidiles was listed first in the original epitaph since it was the first office held. The order of offices held is rearranged for poetic purposes to give the most prestigious offices first.
5 *hec=hic*. The reason for the change in spelling between *hic* in line 4 and *hec* in line 5 is unclear; *hic* replaces the relative pronoun *quei* as in epitaph 1, line 4 and points to a deliberate break with the previous sentence (epitaph 1 puts the titles and

the names of the conquered places in the same sentence); the final m is not written for the accusatives *Corsica Aleriaque urbe.*

6 *Tempestatebus= Tempestatibus: personification of Weather goddesses.*

aide = aidem.

meretod=merito (adverb).

3. Lucius Cornelius Scipio:

This epitaph displays a studied use of archaisms and is remarkable for such literary effects as repetition and alliteration.

1 Proper word order of Scipio's name contrasts with the reworked versions of epitaphs 1b and 2b.

Cornelius ending in *–us*, rather than *–o* as in the original first lines of 1a and 2a.

2 The final m is not written for the accusatives *magna sapientia.* The two nouns and adjectives divide the line into halves.

3 *quom:* archaizing form of *cum.*

saxsum = saxum: spelling encouraged by Accius (contemporary with date of epitaph).

4 *quoiei = cui* (corruption of *quo-* and *qui-* stems).

defecit, non honos honore: a pun on the verb *defecit* used to signify death in the expression *vita defecit,* but also in the expression *honos non defecit* with the sense of "falling short"; repetition and alliteration of *honos, honore; honore* = accusative case— the final m is not written.

5 *quei = qui;* repetitive with *is* but subject of the second idea of the line.

victus est virtutei = alliteration; *virtutei* = dative case: *virtuti.*

6 *annos* with two n's reflects recent spelling.

l[oc]eis = locis.

7 *sit* rather than *siet.*

honore: m missing for the accusative case.

quei = ablative case: *quo.*

sit mandatus: repetition and pun on the sense of *mandatus* from line 6 which signified "to entrust the corpse to the grave/ Hades," but here signifies "to entrust" in the sense of accruing honours; *minus... mandatus: alliteration.*

4. Gnaeus Cornelius Scipio Hispanus:

The two elegiac couplets of this epitaph replace the poetic features of the previous three inscriptions with poetry proper.

1 The correct word order of Hispanus' name, followed by his titles and honours on lines 1 and 2, but separated from the rest of the epitaph to emphasize the poetic treatment of his character.

    pr. = *praetor.*

    aid. cur. = *curule aedile.*

2 *q.* = *quaestor*

    tr. mil II = tribune of soldiers (twice).

    Xvir sl. iudik. = member of the Board of Ten for Judging Lawsuits.

    Xvir sacr. fac. = member of the Board of Ten for Making Sacrifices.

3 *Virtutes*: the elegiac portion of the epitaph begins and ends (*honor*, line 6) with the personal qualities of Hispanus.

    mieis = *meis.*

    accumulavi: first person voice replaces the third person voice of the first three epitaphs.

    Alliteration of m: *carmen*-style effect.

4 Alliteration of p and g: *carmen*-style effect;

    progeniem genui = *figura etymologica*; the line emphasizes three generations of Hispanus' family: his children, his parents, and himself.

5 *sibei* = *sibi.*

    Three elisions; enjambment at end of the line, but all other lines end in a period.

    ut... laetentur: an emphasis on the ancestors' reactions in Hades to the deceased's character.

6 Alliteration of t: *carmen*-style effect.

III. EPIC I: SATURNIAN VERSE

Livius Andronicus

Odyssia

These fragment selections reveal that Livius embellished his Homeric model as often as he compressed narrative details. Book numbers correspond to those of Homer, but due to Livius' adaptation of his model, it is difficult at times to know the precise passage being adapted.

Book 1

1 = *Od.* 1.1:   Ἄνδρα μοι ἔννεπε, Μοῦσα, πολύτροπον . . .

(Text of Thomas W. Allen, *Homeri Opera*, Oxford, 1908, reprinted 1980).

Camena: Homer's muse is replaced by an Italic water goddess. The *Camenae* had a grove outside the Porta Capena, where the Vestals drew their water daily. The *Carmen Priami* contained the line *veteres Casmenas, cascam rem volo profarier* (Varro, *L.L.* 7.28; Morel *FPL*, 29).

insece: imperative; old form of *insequor.*

versutum: perfect passive participle of *verto* and not a compound adjective as we find in the Greek *polytropon.*

2 = *Od.* 1.45; 81:   "ὦ πάτερ ἡμέτερε Κρονίδη . . ."
Minerva (the name that Livius used for Athena does not survive) addresses Jupiter.
Saturni filie: vocative case.

3 = *Od.* 1.64:   "τέκνον ἐμόν, ποῖόν σε ἔπος φύγεν ἕρκος ὀδόντων."
Jupiter to Minerva.
puer = puera

4 = *Od.* 1.137:   καλῇ χρυσείῃ, ὑπὲρ ἀργυρέοιο λέβητος . . .
Minerva (disguised as Mentes) is welcomed into Odysseus' home by Telemachus.
polubro = polubrum, i, neuter; wash-basin.
eclutro = eclutrum, i, neuter; pitcher.

5 = *Od.* 1.169:   "ἀλλ' ἄγε μοι τόδε εἰπὲ καὶ ἀτρεκέως κατάλεξον·"
Telemachus addresses Minerva.
disertim = adverb *plane.*

6 = *Od.* 1.225:   "τίς δαίς, τίς δαὶ ὅμιλος ὅδ' ἔπλετο;"
Athena asks Telemachus about the suitors' feasting.
festus with its religious connotations replaces the generic "gathering" in the Greek.

7 = *Od.* 1.248:   "τόσσοι μητέρ' ἐμὴν μνῶνται, τρύχουσι δὲ οἶκον."
Telemachus describes the suitors.
procitum = petitum (according to Paulus, *ex F.,* 282.3) = to woo – supine with verb of motion.

Book 2

1 = *Od.* 2.422-423:   Τηλέμαχος δ' ἑτάροισιν ἐποτρύνας ἐκέλευσεν
            ὅπλων ἅπτεσθαι·
Telemachus to his crew.
struppis = struppus, i, masculine; a cord.

Book 3

1 = *Od.* 3.110: ἔνθα δὲ Πάτροκλος, θεόφιν μήστωρ ἀτάλαντος . . .
Patroclus is not described here as godlike, as he is in the corresponding *Odyssey* passage, suggesting a cultural preference to shy away from comparing humans to gods. Compare Catullus 11 where *si fas est* is added to his Sapphic model.

2 = *Od.* 2.100: μοῖρ' ὀλοὴ . . .
Penelope speaks about Laertes.
Morta: an Italian deity of death equated with the Greek Moira.
This passage may be an adaptation of *Od.* 3.227-228 where Telemachus
responds to Nestor's hopes for Odysseus' return:
". . . οὐκ 'ν ἐμοί γε
ἐλπομένῳ τὰ γένοιτ', οὐδ' εἰ θεοὶ ὣς ἐθέλοιεν."

Book 4

1 = *Od.* 4.495:　　πολλοὶ μὲν γὰρ τῶν γε δάμεν, πολλοὶ δὲ λίποντο·
Menelaus relates Proteus' report on the Greeks' fate following departure
from Troy.
nequinont = nequeunt.

2 = *Od.* 4.513:　　　　　　　 . . . πότνια "Ηρη.
sancta: Livius embellishes his Homeric model with more solemn lan-
guage.
puer = puera as above.
Saturni filia = Juno.

3 = *Od.* 4.557:　　　　　　. . . νύμφης . . . Καλυψοῦς . . .
Atlantis: use of a patronymic to identify her family.

Book 5

1 = *Od.* 5.297:　　καὶ τότ' 'Οδυσσῆος λύτο γούνατα καὶ φίλον ἦτορ . . .
Description of Ulysses in a storm at sea.
frixit = frigesco, ere, frixi, to become cold.

Book 6

1 = *Od.* 6.142:　　ἦ γούνων λίσσοιτο λαβὼν εὐώπιδα κούρην . . .
Ulysses encounters Nausicaa.
amploctens = amplectens, to clasp in entreaty.

2 = *Od.* 6.295-296: ἔνθα καθεζόμενος μεῖναι χρόνον, εἰς ὅ κεν ἡμεῖς
ἄστυδε ἔλθωμεν καὶ ἱκώμεθα δώματα πατρός.
Nausicaa instructs Ulysses on how to enter the city.
donicum = donec
carpento = carpentum, i, neuter: According to the *Oxford Latin Dictionary*
(OLD), a two wheeled carriage used in Rome, especially by women.

Book 8

1 = *Od.* 8.88: δάκρυ' ὀμορξάμενος κεφαλῆς ἄπο φᾶρος ἔλεσκε . . .
Ulysses weeps while listening to Demodocus sing in Alcinous'
palace.

dacrimas = lacrimas.
noegeo = noegeum, i, neuter; a cloak.

2 = *Od.* 8.138-139: "οὐ γὰρ ἐγώ γέ τί φημι κακώτερον ἄλλο θαλάσσης
ἄνδρα γε συγχεῦαι, εἰ καὶ μάλα καρτερὸς εἴη."
Laodamas speaks.
macerat = macero (1): old meaning of tenderizing meat (soaked in blood?), therefore, a bold metaphor.
topper = toto opere.

3 = *Od.* 8.322-323:   . . . ἦλθ᾽ ἐριούνης
Ἑρμείας, ἦλθεν δὲ ἄναξ ἑκάεργος ᾿Απόλλων.
The gods assemble to witness Mars and Venus chained to Vulcan's bed. Livius drops the gods' Greek epithets.
Latonas: archaic genitive; matronymic reference to Apollo.

4 = *Od.* 8.480-481: ". . . οὕνεκ᾽ ἄρα σφέας
οἴμας Μοῦσ᾽ ἐδίδαξε, φίλησε δὲ φῦλον ἀοιδῶν."
Odysseus describes Demodocus.
Monetas: archaic genitive; Moneta is the Roman equivalent of Mnemosyne, the mother of the Muses. Compare with *Od* 7.480 where money teaches poets.

Book 10

1 = *Od.* 10.64:   "Πῶς ἦλθες, ᾿Οδυσεῦ; τίς τοι κακὸς ἔχραε δαίμων;"
Ulysses relates to Alcinous how Aeolus questioned him. Aeolus, in Livius, does not know whether he is looking at Odysseus or his ghost.
funera: Roman concept of a funeral ceremony used here to signify death.

2 = *Od.* 10.308-309:   ". . . ἐγὼ δ᾽ ἐς δώματα Κίρκης / ἤϊα·"
Odysseus approaches Circe's house.

Book 19

1 = *Od.* 19.225:   χλαῖναν πορφυρέην οὔλην . . .
Ulysses in disguise describes to Penelope a fictional encounter that he had with Ulysses.
pulla: Roman funerary garment, here = adj. "funereal."
Heavy alliteration of p: *carmen*-style effect.

Book 20

1 = *Od.* 20.19-20:   . . . μένος ἄσχετος ἤσθιε Κύκλωψ
ἰφθίμους ἑτάρους·
Warmington (*ROL* II), 40 keeps Priscianus' word order: *cum socios nostros Ciclops impius mandisset.*

Book 21

1 = *Od.* 21.433:   ἀμφὶ δὲ χεῖρα φίλην βάλεν ἔγχεϊ ...
Telemachus arms himself.
suremit = sumit.

Book 22

1 = *Od.* 22.91-93:   ... ἀλλ᾽ ἄρα μιν φθῆ
Τηλέμαχος κατόπισθε βαλὼν χαλκήρεϊ δουρὶ
ὤμων μεσσηγύς, διὰ δὲ στήθεσιν ἔλασσε·
Telemachus slaughters the suitor Amphinomus.

Book 23

1 = *Od.* 23.304-305:   οἳ ἕθεν εἵνεκα πολλά, βόας καὶ ἴφια μῆλα,
ἔσφαζον, πολλὸς δὲ πίθων ἠφύσσετο οἶνος·
Penelope describes the suitors' behaviour to Ulysses.
carnis = nominative case, feminine, singular.
anclabatur = anclo, -are, to serve wine.

Book 24

1 = *Od.* 24.534:   τῶν δ᾽ ἄρα δεισάντων ἐκ χειρῶν ἔπτατο τεύχεα ...
Minerva stops the fighting in Ithaca.

Naevius

Bellum Punicum

The placement of the mythological fragments within books is controversial, although the fusion of mythological and contemporary material within the poem is not.

Book 1
After an invocation to the Muses, the narrative seems to begin with the Roman declaration of war against Carthage, and then shifts to mythological material for the remote cause(s) of the first Punic War. Compare Ennius' opening with Herodotus, who begins his history of the Persian Wars with the series of mythological rapes leading to the Trojan War in order to establish long-standing enmity between Greeks and Asians/Persians.

1* *Novem...sorores*: Livius' Italic *Camenae* are replaced by the Greek Muses.

2* *sagmen, inis,* neuter: a clump of grass plucked by *Fetiales* to become inviolate on foreign soil, therefore a declaration of war against Carthage. Warmington (*ROL* II), 58 places this fragment at the beginning of Book 3, thereby separating the mythological material from the historical content.

3*   Manius Valerius was consul in 263 BCE.

4   Conjectures for the location of this gigantomachy description include a temple frieze on the Temple of Zeus at Agrigento (H. Fränkel, *Hermes* 70 (1935), 59ff.), or a battle shield (E. Fraenkel, *JRS* 44 [1954], 14-17). Strzelecki, xxii-xxiii reviews the evidence for a temple location. Does the theme of Titans versus rebels reflect the theme of Romans versus Carthaginians in the main narrative?

5*   The narrative of events surrounding the fall of Troy and the beginning of Aeneas' journey.
amborum uxores refers to the wives of both Aeneas and Anchises, which contradicts Vergil's version.
operio: to cover.

6   *cum auro* refers to a version of Aeneas' departure from Troy whereby he secured his freedom by betraying the city. This version is known to Livy and alluded to by Vergil.

7*   Servius' notice reveals elements of the Aeneas myth not found in Vergil. As god of thieves and "transferrals" in general, Naevius' mention of Mercury is significant.

8*   *res divas edicit, praedicit castus* is a reference to the prophetic powers Anchises received from Venus.

9*   Another reference to Anchises' prophetic powers.

10*   Anchises prays to Neptune for a safe voyage. The circumlocution emphasizes Jupiter as much as it does Neptune.

11   A reference to Italians whom Aeneas only hears about at this time?

12*   *Cimeria* is the name of the Italian sibyl consulted by Aeneas.

13   *Prochyta* is a kinswoman of Aeneas buried on the island of Procida. This passage reveals Naevius' interest in the Hellenistic verse technique of giving the aetiology of place names.

14*   Macrobius claims that Vergil took this entire passage (*Aeneid* 1.223-296) from Naevius. Despite conflicting myths of Aeneas' departure from Troy and his arrival first in Carthage and then in Italy, Vergil's allusion (a wholesale quotation is unlikely given the length of the passage and Naevius' use of Saturnians) to the *Bellum Punicum* would not contradict his own narrative, since there is no mention of Lavinia or of Aeneas' and Anchises' wives in the Vergilian passage.

15   Servius claims that the whole of Aeneas' speech is taken from a passage in Naevius' *Bellum Punicum:*
> 'O socii (neque enim ignari sumus ante malorum),
> o passi graviora, dabit deus his quoque finem.

> *vos et Scyllaeam rabiem penitusque sonantis*
> *accestis scopulos, vos et Cyclopia saxa*
> *experti: revocate animos maestumque timorem*
> *mittite; forsan et haec olim meminisse iuvabit.*
> *per varios casus, per tot discrimina rerum*
> *tendimus in Latium, sedes ubi fata quietas*
> *ostendunt; illic fas regna resurgere Troiae.*
> *durate, et vosmet rebus servate secundis.'*
> (*Aeneid* 1.198-207, text of R.A.B. Mynors, *P. Vergili Maronis*
> *Opera*, Oxford, 1969).

Since Naevius wrote in Saturnian verse and Vergil in hexameter, this
cannot be a literal quotation of Aeneas' speech in Naevius. Vergil's
allusion to Naevius' text in the form of a speech by Aeneas would
give the *Aeneid* an archaic Latin patina from the outset and possibly
would cast Aeneas as a hybrid Homeric-archaic Latin hero to Vergil's
audience/readers. Since Homer *Od.* 12.208ff. is Naevius' source, we
cannot rule out the possibility that both Naevius and Vergil were
influenced by Livius Andronicus' *Odyssia*.

16 The context of this passage is unclear.

17* Venus addresses Jupiter.
  patrem...supremum optumum is a reference to the Etruscan/Roman
  concept of Jupiter Optimus Maximus.

18* Venus complains to Jupiter.

Book 2

The narrative of Aeneas' adventures following his departure from Troy
continues.

19 *incedit... Proserpina*: Book 2 opens with a council of the gods.

20 *arquitenens = arcitenens:* Macrobius (*Sat.* 6.5.8) claims that the origin
  of this epithet at *Aen.* 3.75: *quam pius Arquitenens* is Naevius' *Bellum*
  Punicum.

21* Although one might assume that Naevius' epic included an account
  of Aeneas' visit to Carthage in order to provide a mythological reason
  for the later enmity between Carthaginians and Romans, this is the
  only extant reference to connect Dido to the poem. Servius' reference
  to Anna's two daughters, named Anna and Dido in Naevius, is not
  found in Vergil. Strezlecki (1964, xxviii) finds echoes of Naevius in
  Dido's suicide speech in which she gives the mythological reason for
  the Punic War:
  > '... *nullus amor populis nec foedera sunto.*
  > *exoriare aliquis nostris ex ossibus ultor*

qui face Dardanios ferroque sequare colonos,
nunc, olim, quocumque dabunt se tempore vires.
litora litoribus contraria, fluctibus undas
imprecor, arma armis: pugnent ipsique nepotesque.'
(*Aen.* 4. 624-629; *OCT* text of Mynors)

22* It is not clear whether the action of the poem has shifted to Italy. This and the next two fragments may refer to Dido's reception of Aeneas, or to Latinus' first encounter with him. Either scenario introduces a level of suspicion on the part of the character meeting Aeneas which is not found in Vergil.

23 *blande et docte percontat*: suggest that the speaker uses guile to obtain information.
quo pacto...liquerit may suggest that the speaker is aware of Aeneas' possible treachery in leaving Troy.

24 The subject of *eius is unclear.*

Book 3

Book 3 seems to cover the period from Aeneas' arrival in Italy to events surrounding the founding of Rome. The extant narrative does not cover any events surrounding Ascanius' founding of Alba Longa. The myths of Aeneas and the founding of Rome (Books 1-3) seem to take up almost half of the *Bellum Punicum*. It is unclear how this earlier material was connected to the more recent historical events of the war beginning in Book 4.

25 *avem aspexit* refers to Anchises taking auspices. If Anchises took these in Italy, then Naevius' version of Aeneas' arrival differs greatly from Vergil's where Anchises dies mysteriously on the way to Carthage, and suggests that in Naevius' version, Anchises was present in Carthage with Aeneas. Were Aeneas' and Anchises' wives also present in Carthage?
ordine emphasizes the ritual character of Anchises' actions and may indicate that he is setting precedents for later Roman religion.

26 *Amulius:* the brother of Numitor (grandfather of Romulus and Remus) who cheated Numitor of the throne.
susum= sursum: upwards.

27* If *nepotem* here means grandson (rather than a descendant), then Servius' notice offers a variant of the identity of Romulus' and Remus' mother, and indicates that Naevius' chronologically compressed narrative did not include the Alban Kings. Various names given to the mother of the twins include: Rhea, Rhea Silvia, Ilia, Aemilia, or Servilia.

28* *Balatium* seems to be Naevius' word for the Palatine Hill and reveals the Hellenistic literary technique of offering the aetiology of a place within a narrative. Sander M. Goldberg, *Epic in Republican Rome* (Oxford, 1995), 54 ff., however, cautions against reading Vergilian Alexandrianism back into Naevius.

29* *Aventinum:* Servius' notice again illustrates Naevius' interest in Hellenistic narrative technique by offering the aetiology of the Aventine Hill. These two hills played an important role in the twins' taking of the auspices to determine who would name and rule Rome. Unfortunately, there are no extant fragments describing the contest.

Book 4

An account of the first Punic War begins.

30* Cichorius (1922, 24 ff). reconstructs the passage: *Navali corona...* *<Primus eam accepit C.> Atilius bel<lo Punico primo, ut a Naevio narra>tum est in car<mine Belli Punici>.*

C. Atilius was awarded the crown for his naval victory.

31* Samnite: Naevius used the unconventional neuter form *hoc Samnite* to refer to a Samnite. The context of this passage may be the Samnite slave revolt in 259 BCE.

32 *Melitam* = Malta.
urit, populatur, vastat ...: The pile-up of verbs suggests the cruel efficiency of the Roman army.

33 The taking of auspices.

34 *virum* may be corrupt for *verum.*
auspicat auspicium = figura etymologica.

35 *danunt = dant*

36 Alliteration of v: *carmen*-style effect.

Book 5

No fragments can be assigned to Book 5.

Book 6

37 A reference to Publius Claudius Pulcher (consul 249)?

38 Terms of the treaty between the Romans and Hiero of Syracuse.

39 *ilico = in eo loco.*
s.edent refers to Romans? Does a Carthaginian speak this line about the Romans in a council of Carthaginian generals?

40 Is the subject of *censet* a Roman general?

Book 7

The narrative covers C. Lutatius Catulus' naval victory at the Aegates Islands and the peace settlement of 241 BCE.

41* *onerariae* = cargo ships.

42* *paciscit* = *pacisco,* to arrange by negotiation, in particular of an award or compensation.

43 This corrupt passage seems to refer to the terms of Catulus' treaty following the Roman victory at the Aegates Islands.

44* This notice is important for many reasons. First, according to the literary historian Varro, Naevius was the first poet to be paid for a poem. Secondly, Naevius mentions this fact within the poem itself, presumably at the very end in a *sphragis*, a poetic seal in the Hellenistic tradition, by which a poet identifies himself in the body of the poem, as Vergil does at the end of the *Georgics.* Naevius also left a record of his literary accomplishments in his epitaph (in Saturnians):

> *Inmortales mortales si foret fas flere,*
> *Flerent divae Camenae Naevium poetam.*
> *Itaque postquam est Orchi traditus thesauro,*
> *Obliti sunt Romae loquier lingua Latina.*

Fragmenta Incertae Sedis

58 *arquitenens* This is the second appearance of this epithet. cf. Book 2, fragment 20.

IV. TRAGEDY I

Livius Andronicus

Aegisthus

1 Alliteration of p: *carmen*-style effect.

2 This is an intentionally poetic description of dolphins.

3 Are these lines spoken to Clytemnestra by Agamemnon as he steps down from his chariot, or to Clytemnestra by an unknown character as she beholds the corpse of Agamemnon?

4 *rumino* (1) = (of cattle) to chew food. This is the earliest extant figurative use of the word to signify "to turn over in one's mind." An example of Livius' poetic innovations.

5 Alliteration of l and t: *carmen*-style effect.

6　natae: Could Iphegenia still be alive at this point?

7　Agamemnon falls to the ground rather forcefully.

8　The concept of *maiestas* is Roman rather than Greek.

Tereus

1　The speaker is unknown.

2　Tereus speaking to himself?

3　This line must follow a speech by Procne stating her resolve to exact vengeance for Tereus' rape of her sister.

4　*limo* (1) = to rub smooth with a file, which in the context of kissing, is quite graphic and innovative. This is the earliest extant use of the word which later took on the figurative meaning of polishing (of a work of literature).

Naevius

Danae

1　*valentia, ae* = power. This is the earliest extant use of the word.

2　Whatever the tone of the passage, it seems that Danae stands silently on stage while Acrisius (?) addresses person(s) unknown. Here, Ribbeck has changed the manuscript reading of *contemplo* to *contempla* which may further change the tone of the passage.

5　A euphemism for sex? The mingling of hand with water (Jupiter) recalls a Roman wedding ceremony. The alliteration of m suggests the flowing of water.

7　The alliteration of q and p evoke a solemn announcement as Acrisius (?) passes judgment.

9　A reference to Semele, the mother of Dionysus, possibly offered as a reason why she yielded to Jupiter.

10　*suppetias (suppetiae, arum)* = come to one's aid. This is the earliest extant use of the word.

11　*fulgurio* (4) = to cause lightning. This is the first extant use of this verb.

Lycurgus

3　*liberi* = masculine.

4　*suavisonum* is an expression coined by Naevius.

5　*frundiferos* is an expression coined by Naevius.

7   The alliteration of l suggests the flapping of wings and the near repetition of words evokes haste. The comparison of the Maenads to birds appears in Euripides' *Bacchae*.

8   *vitulor, -ari* = rejoicing. First extant use of the word.

9   *Bacchae, Bacchico* = near repetition of noun and adjectival forms and alliteration of c.
    schema, atis, neuter = an outfit: a Greek borrowing first used by Naevius.

12 A line heavy with alliteration of a and elision.

18 *patagium, ii,* neuter = border on a woman's tunic (Greek?), here = robe by metonymy. This is the first extant use of the word.
    crocota, ae = (Greek) saffron-coloured dress; first extant use of the word.
    malacus, a , um = (Greek) soft; first extant use of the word.

20 Alliteration of v and f.

21 This line refers to the punishment of Lycurgus which seems to form the denouement of the play.

Incerti Nominis Reliquiae

4   This line seems to belong to this play as a description of Liber.
    diabathrum, i, neuter = (Greek) slipper; first extant use of the word.
    epicrocum, i, neuter = (Greek) sheer yellow robe; first extant use of the word.

Ennius

Alexander

1   The first two lines are spoken about Cassandra and are followed by a *canticum*.
    mater, optumatum multo mulier melior mulierum: Ennius loads the line with *carmen*-style elements: heavy alliteration of m, the repetition of *mulier* and the near rhyme of *mulier* and *melior* for maximum aural effect.
    hariolatio, onis, feminine = prophecy, first extant use of the word.
    fatis fandis = figura etymologica.
    Virgines....: alliteration of v, p, and m = *carmen*-style effect.
    Optumam = the third time a variation of this adjective is used in this speech. Alliteration of p in this line.
    men obesse, illos prodesse, // me obstare, illos obsequi = versus

quadratus: two clauses on each side of the caesura, each with an accusative subject (first letter m, i, alternating), and infinitive (each of three syllables).

2 *fax:* Cassandra prophesizes in metaphorical language.

3 Cassandra continues to describe her vision.
Note the heavy alliteration of m, c, v and l = *carmen*-style effect.
classis cita/ texitur = onomatopoeic.
velivolans, antis, adjective = expression coined by Ennius.

4 Cassandra describes the judgment of Paris.

5 See Jocelyn, 221, for Ennius' adaptation of Greek sacrificial language for a Roman audience expressed in contemporary Roman terms.
facem: continuation of torch metaphor first used in fragment 2.
balantibus recalls Naevius' initial use of the word in the *Bellum Punicum* as an *aitia* to account for the name Palatine.
postulat pacem petens: alliteration of p = *carmen*-style effect.
puerum primus Priam: further alliteration of p.
eum esse exitium Troiae, pestem Pergamo = the harsh elisions at the beginning of the line emphasize the idea of destruction. The alliteration of p in the final two words give further emphasis to the high number of p's used throughout.

6 Heavy assonance of a.

7 Ennius includes a Hellenistic *aition* on the origin of the name Paris.

8 A description of Alexander's beauty? If this fragment refers to the hitherto unknown Alexander's entry as a contestant, perhaps *amicto* should be supplied, "...in his cloak he was flawless and beautiful...."

9 A reference to Alexander's uneducated childhood among shepherds?

10 *volans:* a metaphor for victory or an actual stage description of the goddess Victory. The prologue of Euripides' play was spoken by Aphrodite. See Jocelyn (1967, 230) who argues for a prologue spoken by Victory in Ennius' play.

11 *paupertas:* just as in Caecilius Statius where a reference to the poor, versus the rich, was added to the Greek original, Ennius here emphasizes the connection between poverty and obscurity, which as a poet in the service of patrons he understood well.

12 Cassandra predicts Hector's death as related in the *Iliad*.
respectantibus...nobis: the emphasis on the act of watching, rather than the action itself, anticipates Senecan drama.

13 Cassandra describes the Trojan Horse.

Medea Exul

1   Based on the opening lines of Euripides' play, this speech formed the
opening lines of Ennius' play. This conjecture is based on Cicero's
quotation of the passage at *de Nat. Deo.* 3.75. See further, arguments in
Jocelyn (1967, 350). Ennius, however, alters the opening lines of Eu-
ripides' play in several ways. He lists the events of the Argo's voyage
chronologically; he omits the detail that the Argive heroes rowed the
ship themselves, thereby making their social station comprehensible
to a Roman audience; and he changes the Argo's timber from pine to
fir, which was in contemporary use in Rome. Ennius adapted rather
than adopted Euripides' text. On the dangers of comparing Ennius'
play with Euripides', see Jocelyn (1967, 347): "Similarity with the text
of Euripides' *Medea* is a quite treacherous guide. Study of Nonius'
quotations of the *Hecuba* shows that Ennius departed radically from
the wording of his original even more than he adhered to it."
utinam... : heavy alliteration of n = *carmen*-style effect.
abiegna: Romans used fir rather than pine as used in Greece, therefore
Ennius adapts his Greek original for a Roman audience.
caesa accidisset: the alliteration of c emphasizes the sound of cutting
a tree.
nominatur nomine = figura etymologica.
Argo: Ennius gives the etymology of the name.
...Argivi...delecti viri = aristocrats who do not row as they do in Eu-
ripides' version, therefore another alteration for a Roman audience.
era errans: repetition of sounds but words are unrelated.
domo: In Euripides' play the emphasis is on the arrival to Iolcus,
rather than the departure from Colchis as it is here.
animo aegro amore: assonance of a
saevo saucia: alliteration of s.
The Nurse's speech is eliminated by Seneca in his *Medea*, where he
emphasizes the marriage between Jason and Medea by having Medea
deliver the prologue herself.

2   Fragment 2 seems to correspond to the scene in Euripides' play in
which Medea confronts Jason (lines 465-519), but curiously, Ennius
uses the conversational trimeter, rather than typical musically-ac-
companied verse which one would expect in such a highly emotional
scene.
quo...: a series of rhetorical questions which point to Medea's hopeless
situation, since her previous crimes prevent her from returning home
or to the court of King Pelias.

3   In fragment 3, Medea addresses the matrons of Corinth, rather than
the generic women found in Euripides. The first line is omitted in
Jocelyn's text for metrical reasons. I include it as a line which may

be corrupt but which essentially preserves the context of the lost original, especially the elevated social and married status of Medea's addressees and their domicile on an *arx*, which corresponds to the Palatine Hill in Rome. The highly alliterative *sententiae*, following Medea's address, express Roman ideas of foreign *provinciae*, typical of the assignments given to contemporary magistrates, again showing adaptation rather than translation.

Quae... matronae opulentae optimates: Ennius makes it clear that Medea is addressing her social equals, expressed in terms intelligible to Romans, rather than generic women as in Euripides' version. The Corinthian women, however, are legal wives (*matronae*), whereas the foreign Medea is not (*concubina*). Cicero, who preserves this passage (*Fam.* 7.6.1), describes Medea as having powdered limbs (*manibus gypsatissimis*); thus Ennius further emphasizes Medea's foreign status among the Corinthians and even his own contemporary Roman audience, the women of which did not wear cosmetics at this date.

arcem altam: topography of Rome is alluded to here to equate the Corinthian rich with the Roman elite who lived on the Palatine Hill.

suam rem...publicam: the emphasis on duty here is an adaption of the Greek text which stresses the notion of public shame.

publicam patria procul: heavy alliteration emphasizes the solemn tone of Medea's address.

4   *sapiens...sapit/ quit nequiquam = figurae etymologicae* which point to Medea's sophistry.

5   *Medeai* = archaic genitive.

7   *blandiloquentia:* a phrase coined by Ennius.

9   *repagulum, i, ae* = door-bars, the graphic image is used figuratively, possibly for the first time in Latin literature, by Ennius.

     mihi maerores, illi luctum,// exitium illi, exilium mihi. This is a *versus quadratus* with a caesura following *luctum*. The first half of the line balances the datives *mihi* and *illi* with the direct objects *maerores* and *luctum*. The second half of the line reverses the order of the datives and lists the direct objects first: ABCD//DCBA. Note the near rhyme of *exitium* and *exilium*. The mastery of the *carmen*-style in this line undercuts Ennius' criticisms of Livius' and Naevius' poetry.

12   *antiqua erilis fida custos corporis:* an elaborate address to the Nurse.

13   Heavy elision and alliteration in both lines.

14 *cette manus vestrea measque accipite:* the syntax reinforces the idea of the mixing of hands and recalls the handshake of treaties, ironic for the children, who do not suspect that their mother will soon kill them.

16 *cordis cupido corde:* an almost double *figura etymologica* with the repetition of words signalling desire.

V. EPIC II – HEXAMETER VERSE

Ennius

Annales

Book 1

After an invocation to the Muses, Book 1 covers the events from Aeneas' departure from Troy to Romulus' deification.

1 *Musae* are invoked rather than the Camenae of Livius' *Odyssia* and Naevius' epitaph. This may not be the actual first line of the poem (cf. Skutsch, 143-144).

2 *somno... revinctus:* this recalls Hesiod's and Callimachus' encounters with the Muses. See Skutsch, 147-153 for ancient testimonia and imitations of this passage, in particular on the connection between Ennius' encounter with the Muses and the narrative of Homer's metempsychosis as Ennius.

3 *Homerus:* Ennius claims that Homer appeared to him in a dream.

4 Lucretius seems to follow Ennius closely here. After a description of the shades of the departed to explain how Homer communicates with Ennius, Homer reveals *rerum natura* to him. Homer sheds tears upon seeing Ennius, but whether these are tears of joy or grief is controversial. See Skutsch, 154-157, who favours tears of grief.

5 Homer addresses Ennius.

6 *pavom=* peacock. This is a symbol of reincarnation in Pythagorean thought. It seems that Homer not only inspired Ennius to write the *Annales* but that Ennius via the peacock is actually the reincarnation of Homer. Horace alludes to this passage at *Ep.* 2.1.50-52:

> *Ennius et sapiens et fortis et alter Homerus*
> *ut critici dicunt, leviter curare videtur*
> *quo promissa cadant et somnia Pythagorea.*
> (*OCT* text of E.C. Wickham, 1901, repr. 1959)

The phrase *alter Homerus* was coined by Lucilius (Hieronymus, *comment. in Micham* lib II cap 7: *Homerus alter ut Lucilius de Ennio suspicatur*).

7 *poemata:* Ennius uses a Hellenized word to denote poetry.

8 *doctus... Anchisesque...:* Ennius, like Naevius, attributes prophetic powers to Anchises. It is unclear whether Anchises is mentioned here in connection with Aeneas' departure from Troy.

9 *est locus...:* this is the first extant use of this construction which Latin authors used to remove the narrative from its present context to another one.
Hesperiam: together with *Saturnia terra* in the next line, is a mythological name for Italy.
mortales perhibebant: Does this mean that the gods call it by another name? It is unclear whether this passage forms a prophecy (to Aeneas or to the reader) about Italy.

10 *Saturnia terra* seems to refer specifically to Latium through the Etruscan god Saturn and his temple at the foot of the Capitoline Hill, rather than to Italy.

11 *Prisci...Latini:* the ancient tribe of Italians encountered by Aeneas. The *Prisci Latini* are also mentioned by Cato, *Origines* 1.5, and Livy, *A.U.C.* 1.1.5, etc., as the original inhabitants of Latium.

cascus,a,um = ancient.

12/13 Does Ennius introduce a brief theogony here?

Caelus = masculine for Ouranos. See Courtney (*FLP*, 30) for comparisons with the fragments from Ennius' *Euhemerus*.

14 *Teque pater Tiberine:* Aeneas prays to Tiber. Vergil adapts this line: *tuque, o Thybri tuo genitor cum flumine sancto* (*Aen.* 8.72).

15 *pium Anchisen:* Could Aeneas be describing his ancestors to Latinus or Evander?

16 *quos homines* refers to the arrival of the Trojans.

17 *rex Albai Longai:* the narrative between Aeneas' arrival to Italy and Ascanius' (?) founding of the Alban line does not survive. It is not clear which Alban king is the speaker.

18 These are the terms for a formal treaty between Aeneas and the Alban king, which Vergil evokes at *Aen.* 8.150 when Aeneas enters into a treaty with Evander: *accipe daque fidem.*

19 This fragment describes the dream of Ilia (mother of Romulus and Remus). Ennius does not name Ilia – a Hellenistic literary device.

Ilia addresses this speech to her old nurse (*Eurydica prognata*). See Gordon Williams, *Tradition and Originality* (Oxford, 1968, 690) for an analysis of the temporal connectives in this passage.

homo pulcer: a reference to Mars?

locos novos: not trodden on by humans before, as with *semita nulla.*

postilla = postea.

errare videbar recalls *Aen.* 4.465-473, where Dido's trance-like dream is described, especially the expression *videtur/ ire* (4.467-468): "... *semper longam incomitata videtur/ ire viam et Tyrios deserta quaerere terra.*"

gerendae aerumnae: "toils" — a reference to her pregnancy with twins and her imprisonment.

post ex fluvio fortuna resistet refers to her eventual marriage with the river Tiber and her transformation into a sea goddess.

pater: referring to the *homo pulcer.*

corde cupitus approximates a *figura etymologica.*

ad...templa: the regions of the sky used for augury.

lacrumans = lacrimans.

voce vocabam = figura etymologica.

20 *cenacula maxuma caeli* refers to a council of the gods.

21 *Iuno Saturnia*: this epithet emphasizes Juno's equal status with her brother(s) and appears later in Vergil with the same emphasis.

22 *unus erit quem tu tolles* refers to the deification of Romulus, and may occur in the speech of Juno rather than in a speech in response. Juno makes a similar statement concerning Romulus in Horace, *Carm.* 3.30, but in Vergil, *Aen.* 12.808-829, Juno does not refer to Romulus. Julius Caesar was the second Roman ever deified, before deifications became common under the Empire.

23 The account of Ilia's death and marriage to Tiber does not survive.

24 Ilia (?) addressing Venus. The use of *cognata* in an address to a god is unusual.

25 It is not clear who is addressing Ilia.

26 *lupus femina:* the exposure of the twins. Details of the childhood of the twins, found in Livy, do not survive.

27 The fragments resume with the contest beween Romulus and Remus. The language and images emphasize Remus' isolation and his defeat.

Curantes magna cum cura: repetitious.

auspicio augurioque: the similar meanings give a *versus quadratus* effect for a solemn tone to the passage.

in monte = Murcus, part of the Aventine Hill.

Remus: the name of Remus occurs only once in the nominative (versus twice for Romulus).

solus: emphasizes Remus' isolation.

avem: the mention of a single bird here anticipates the outcome. Did Remus aim too low in his expectations?

Romulus pulcer: Remus was not given an adjective and the choice of *pulcer* (handsome, manly, courageous) seems to single Romulus out for success.

Aventino: there is much discrepancy regarding the respective hills. Servius, *ad Aen* 3.46 preserves the story of Romulus throwing a spear onto the Palatine from the Aventine. Other authors put Romulus on the Palatine and Remus on the Aventine. See T.P. Wiseman, *Remus* (Cambridge, 1995) for the historiographic tradition surrounding the twins.

genus altivolantum = birds.

Certabant...vocarent: the contest was over ruling Rome, but Ennius elegantly presents the conflict as one of naming rather than of fighting.

Romam Remoramne: Rome is mentioned first, emphasizing the oddity of the second name.

uter here, as with *utri* below, Ennius assigns suspense on the part of the onlookers even while his narrative betrays the winner.

induperator = archaic for *imperator*, leaving no doubt as to the stakes involved in the contest.

Exspectant veluti: Ennius, unlike Homer, uses an urban metaphor to describe the crowd's anticipation even though the urban setting (circus) and context (chariot racing) alluded to do not yet exist.

consul: the term was not used until the fifth century; it should be *praeter* or *praeter maximus* (see Festus, 152 L).

quom = *cum.*

ad carceris oras = the starting gate.

e faucibus = from the starting gate.

populus: Livy states that only obscure and lowly types comprised the original populace of Rome (*A.U.C.* 1.8).

magni victoria... regni: the true prize of the contest becomes more obvious as the passage progresses. Calling the kingdom great is anachronistic, since its greatness lies ahead at the time of the passage.

sol albus = sun setting the night before the taking of the auspices, signalling an abrupt transition to the next line.

simul, repeated on the next line, suggests that Remus should have waited rather than seeking an omen exactly at sunrise.

pulcerrima praepes...avis adds a level of suspense as to the outcome until Romulus' omen is announced. *Avis* echoes *avem* above, suggest-

ing that, ironically (or deservedly), Remus got what he hoped for.
aureus sol = sun.

corpora sancta implies divine favour.

praepetibus...pulcrisque locis: a *versus quadratus* effect which calls
attention to Remus' lesser omen as well as to the description of Ro-
mulus as *pulcer.*

propitim = specifically.

scamna = throne, which makes it clear that only one king can win.

28 The context of this fragment is the quarrel over the wall, but it is not
clear whether Romulus or Remus is the speaker.
Iuppiter: either the subject of another verb or an exclamation.

quamde = quam.

29 Romulus on the point of killing Remus for jumping over his new city
wall. Livy, *A.U.C.* 1.7.2, rejects this version of Remus' death and states
that Remus was killed following the taking of the auspices, but under
suspicious circumstances: *ibi in turba ictus Remus cecidit.*

30 The scholiast notice states that Romulus built the Temple of Jupiter
Feretrius which was the oldest temple of Rome. The reference to
ludi (boxing and chariot racing) may indicate a narrative diversion
following the contest and Remus' death. Livy claims that Romulus
dedicated the Temple of Jupiter Feretrius following his victory over
Caenina, but it is not clear from Ennius' fragments whether the *ludi*
here were, perhaps, part of Remus' funeral games.

31 †*Virgines* = Sabine women.

32 Hersilia seems to be the speaker but the context of the passage is
unclear.

33 This highly alliterative line (spoken by Romulus?) alludes to the death
of the Sabine king Titus Tatius who ruled jointly with Romulus.

34 *Romulus in caelo:* following Romulus' deification, his name was
changed to Romulus-Quirinus. It is significant that Book 1 of the
Annales is framed by metamorphoses: Ennius' metempsychosis and
Romulus' apotheosis. If Book 1 contained mostly mythological mate-
rial, then the apotheosis of Romulus provides a bridge to the historical
material beginning in Book 2.

Book 2

The narrative covers the reigns of Numa Pompilius, Tullus Hostilius, and
Ancus Marcius.

1 *Olli* = Numa. Roman legend believed that Numa communicated with

the nymph Egeria (*suavis sonus*). Later writers, especially Juvenal, cast their relationship as a sexual one.
Egeriai = genitive.

2 Numa's religious reforms.
ancilia = sacred shields.
liba = sacrificial cakes.
fictores = attendants to priests whose roles were later assumed by Vestals.
tutulatos = headbands?

3 A continuation of Numa's religious reforms. Here six of the twelve *flamines minores* are listed.

4 *quid...humanitus* = neuter. This line seems to come from a speech by Numa referring to his status after death.

5 *Mettoeoque Fufetioeo* = Mettius Fufetius, who was convicted of treason under Tullus Hostilius. Livy, *A.U.C.* 1.28, claims that he was the only Roman ever punished by quartering.

6 *Horatius:* the story of the three Horatii fighting against the Curiatii is preserved in Livy, *A.U.C.* 1. 24-25. This line may refer to the last fighting Horatius. If, however, this is a reference to Horatius Cocles, this fragment should be in Book 4, not in Book 2. The placement of this fragment here interrupts the narrative of Mettius' punishment.

7 *tractatus*= Mettius' quartered body.

8 *miserum...homonem*= *hominem*, refers to Mettius.
crudeli sepulchro= vultures' bodies.

9 *Cael>i*= Caelian Hill where the Albans settled following the destruction of Alba Longa.

10 *Ostia:* this served as Rome's seaport and was also the site of important salt mines, the construction of which was attributed to Ancus Marcius.

Book 3

Book 3 describes the reigns of the Tarquins and it is likely that the book ended with their expulsion and the founding of the Republic.

1 *Postquam....*: following the death of Ancus, Tarquinius Priscus became king.
sis = *suis*.
This line is borrowed by Lucretius, *DRN* 3.1025.

2 *Tarquinio* = Tarquinius Priscus, who arrived at Rome as a foreigner named Lucumo, as Livy relates in *A.U.C.*1.34.

3 The portent of an eagle landing on Priscus is found in Livy, *A.U.C.* 1.34.

aera = aer: a philosophical intrusion in the narrative?

4 Skutsch, 300: "Virgil's story of the flames seen on the head of Iulus, Anchises' prayer for confirmation of the favourable omen, and the answering clap of thunder on the left, *Aen.* 2.679ff., is evidently based on a similar scene in the *Annals*, Iulus and Anchises having replaced Servius Tullius and Tanaquil [...]." Livy, *A.U.C.* 1.39ff, narrates the events surrounding Priscus' portent.

5 *Olli* = to Tanaquil, wife of Priscus, who was instrumental in securing the throne for him as well as for their chosen successor, Servius Tullius.

6 *bona femina* = Tanaquil.

Book 4

Book 4 covers events surrounding the early Republic and its restoration following the Gallic disaster.

1 The speaker asks whether another aims to usurp power. The usurper may be Sp. Maelius.

2 Skutsch, 314-316, suggests that Ennius imagines a date for Rome's founding, by Aeneas' grandson Romulus, around 1100 BCE (Eratosthenes had placed the date of Troy's fall at 1184 BCE). Subtracting 700 years would place this fragment in the context of Camillus' rejection of the relocating of Romans to Veii, around 400 BCE.

Augusto augurio = carmen-style effect.

Book 5

Events covered in this book include the execution of the Younger Manlius in 340 BCE and battles surrounding Rome's Italic neighbors.

1 *res Romana = res publica.*

moribus emphasizes the austere morality of the early Romans.

2 *Campani* = incorporation of more Italians into the urban population of Rome.

Book 6

This book covers events surrounding the war against King Pyrrhus.

1 *Quis...*: a short proem such as we find at the beginning of Book 10.

2 A reference to King Pyrrhus which emphasizes his Greek origins as a descendant of the Aeacids.

3 *Burrus* = Pyrrhus.
a stirpe supremo: as an Aeacid, Pyrrhus claimed descent from Achilles' son Neoptolemus. Aeacus was Peleus' father.

4 *Aio:* the Delphic oracle predicting the outcome of the Roman war against Pyrrhus, but the double meaning here depends upon which accusative (*te* or *Romanos*) is taken as the subject of the infinitive *posse.*

5 After the battle of Heraclea.

6 Ennius takes the opportunity to display his poetic skill by describing the felling of trees for funeral pyres. Notice the wide variety of trees, the active and passive verbs, and the emphasis on sound through alliteration. This passage is based on Homer, *Iliad* 23.117-120 and later is emulated by Vergil, *Aen.* 6.179-182; Silius Italicus, *Punica* 10.527-534; Statius *Thebaid* 6.90-107.

7 Pyrrhus speaks to Fabricius, who proposes the ransom of prisoners following the Battle of Heraclea. Lines are used to arrange syntax, thereby adding precision to Pyrrhus' points and adding a dignified air to his speech.
nec mi aurum posco // nec mi pretium dederitis: the first line of the speech is a *versus quadratus* divided perfectly in two, with identical elements in the same order in each half.
cauponantes = *cauponor,ari* = to trade in something (*caupo* = an inn or a shopkeeper).
belligerentes = warriors, not profiteers.
era = Lady Luck.
quorum virtuti = to whose courage
Dono, ducite, doque = *carmen*-style effect. Here, rather than using three verbs with similar meanings, Ennius frames *ducite* with two verbs of similar meaning.
magnis dis: this is a common line-ending in Vergil's *Aeneid*, indicating that Vergil uses archaisms throughout his poem.

Book 7

Book 7 covers events from the First Punic War to the Second Punic War. Ennius begins with a major proem, as he does in Books 1 and 16. Skutsch, 367, argues that Books 1-6 may have been published already. Here, Ennius either treats briefly or ignores the events surrounding the First Punic War, since they had already been described by Naevius.

1 *alii* refers to Livius and Naevius. Ennius here touts the superiority of his hexameters over the native Italian Saturnian.
vorsibus = *versibus.*
Faunei vatesque refer disparagingly to Livius and Naevius. Ennius

makes a statement on the antiquity of Saturnians versus the modernity of the hexameter.

2 *Musarum scopulos* = Mount Helicon, where Hesiod encountered the Muses, therefore, poetic inspiration.
dicti studiosus = a knowledge of Greek Hellenistic verse techniques.
reserare = to unlock. A bold metaphor to describe Ennius' daring and talent in revealing the potential of Latin poetry, which he suggests remained hidden from his precursors Livius and Naevius.

3 Ennius seems to make the claim that, despite his encounter with Homer, he is not a newcomer to philosophy and poetry. Such a defence of his dream in Book 1 suggests that Books 1-6 had already been published.
sapientia = the Latin translation for the Greek *sophia*.
sam = *eam* (philosophy).

4 *Poeni:* a reference to the Carthaginian practice of sacrificing the first-born child, which also serves to paint the enemy in a barbaric light.

5 *Appius* = Appius Claudius Caudex as he enters Sicily.

6 *Paluda virago* = Discordia, which Ennius describes in Empedoclean terms for strife.

7 This fragment describes the escape of vapours from the Underworld in the valley of the Nar.
sulpureas = sulphur, an expression coined by Ennius.

8 *cupressi... buxum:* Ennius makes these trees masculine and may describe the Plutonium. Evergreens were often associated with funereal contexts.

9 Discordia breaks open the gates of War (associated at this time with the Temple of Janus?). Servius claims that *Aen.* 7.622 *belli ferratos* is a variation of Ennius' highly alliterative line.

10 The Marsi, Paeligni, and the Vestini were faithful allies of Rome. Ennius varies the word for 'company' and uses alliteration in only two of the three cola. The hardiness of Italic stock seems reflected in the rhythm and the lengthening cola of the line.

11 These words come from a speech Hannibal made before crossing the Alps. Ennius changes the traditional proverb *fortes fortuna adiuvat* (Terence, *Phorm.* 203) to emphasize alliteration. Macrobius (*Sat.* 6.1.62) compares *Aen.* 10.284: *audentes fortuna iuvat*, which Turnus speaks, with Ennius' line.

12 *quadrupes* emphasizes the exotic nature of the animals used by Hannibal, and may refer to the battle of Trebia.

13 The names of the gods seem randomly given, but on closer inspection we find the names of female and male gods divided on separate lines, except for Mars who is placed significantly next to Venus. All 12 gods are connected with the expiatory rite known as the *lectisternium* (a procession of the gods on couches), and this fragment seems to allude to one such rite performed in 217 BCE during the Hannibalic War.

Book 8

Book 8 narrates events surrounding the Hannibalic War.

According to Priscianus, (ap GL II, 209, GK), Ennius inserted a reference to Dido in Book 8, perhaps to connect the Carthaginian War with his earlier narrative of Dido and Aeneas: *Dido, Didonis...Ennius in VIII Poenos Didone oriundos.*

1 Aemilius Paullus seems to be the speaker of this line warning that an unsuccessful turn of events may unexpectedly follow a successful one.

2 Note the alliteration of s and the force of *quatit ungula terram.*

3 This passage describes the companion (*contubernalis*) of C. Servilius Geminus in terms which seem to describe Ennius himself (in particular, the catalogue of qualities) and his own relationship with his patron M. Fulvius Nobilior.
Haece locutus: Geminus has just finished delivering a speech.
summis rebus regendis = important affairs of state.
indu = in.
faceret facinus = *figura etymologica.*
doctus = learned in a Hellenistic sense.
verbum paucum = *verborum paucorum* "of few words."
Serilius = Ennius condenses Servilius' name for metrical purposes.

4 Ennius included the gods as audience/participants in Roman affairs outside of Book 1, as Jupiter's promise to Juno of the defeat of Carthage reveals.

5 According to Skutsch, 466, "Juno's change of mind must have occurred between Cannae and the major successes of Rome, the capture of Syracuse, the fall of Capua and Tarentum, and the battle of Metaurus." Livius Andronicus composed a *partheneion* in 207 BCE, consisting of 27 virgins, to appease Juno (cf. Livy, *A.U.C.* 27.37.7-15).

Book 9

A continuing account of events surrounding the Hannibalic War.

1 *Cethegus:* just as in the archaizing inscription of Scipio, Cathegus' full name is given here in a random order and resembles the rearrangement of Lucius Cornelius Scipio Barbatus' epitaph. His full name is Marcus Cornelius f. Marci Cethegus.
flos delibatus = plucked flower.
Suadaique medulla = the quintessence of eloquence.

Book 10

The narrative of the Macedonian War begins with a short proem.

1 *Musa:* an invocation to the Muse to recount the details of battle.

Book 11

The fragments from this book cannot be placed in secure contexts, but they seem to describe the Roman victory over Philip and the declaration of freedom for Greece at the Isthmian Games in 196 BCE.

Book 12

The two main events treated in this book seem to be the campaign against Nabis of Sparta and the victories in Spain (195 BCE) of Ennius' former patron, Cato.

1 *Unus homo... cunctando* refers to Fabius Maximus Cunctator.

Noenum = *non.*

2 This fragment describes the actions of an army following a victory, but it is unclear which army is meant.

mortales = *homines.*

Book 13

Outbreak of the Syrian War.

1 A reference to the bridge constructed by Xerxes to cross into Europe.
Hellesponto pontem = pun.

2 King Antiochus reports the advice of Hannibal not to wage war against Rome, but to harrass while he extended the war to Italy.
quem: refers to Hannibal, not *cor.*

3 Hannibal (?) disparages the effectiveness of *vates* in giving or following reliable advice as it pertains to their own lives.
verant = to tell the truth.

Book 14

Various battles are described.

1   An onomatopoeic line describing a ship moving at great speed.
volat super = tmesis.

2   A description of a fleet setting out suddenly, but the context is unclear.
Skutsch, 542-543, suggests the battle off Corycus in 191 BCE, the
battle of Myonnesus in 190 BCE, or (following Merula) the crossing
of the Hellespont by the Roman army.
marmore flavo describes the colour of foam and contrasts with the
colour of the sea (*caeruleum*).

3   A reference to the battle of Myonnessus (?) fought between the Syr-
ians and the Romans/Rhodians.
velivolis: of ships.

4   Battle-drawn soldiers (at battle of Magnesia?) "bristle."

5   The cremation of the Roman dead following the battle of Magnesia?
in nocte serena: Ennius places the cremations at night for dramatic
effect rather than to reflect Roman custom, which did not require
cremations at night.

Book 15

Description of Nobilior's Aetolian campaign and the siege of Ambracia.

1   It is significant that Ennius ended his original version of the *Annales*
with the triumph of his patron and the entry of the Muses into the Ro-
man pantheon. By making Nobilior's campaign the last episode in the
epic, Ennius suggests that it is the culmination of all previous Roman
history. This teleological approach to myth and history, which we also
find in Ovid's *Metamorphoses*, distinguishes Roman narratives from
Greek ones. Ennius also treated the campaign in an earlier *praetexta*,
Ambracia, which he wrote for Nobilior. Did he end Book 15 with a
sphragis, perhaps mentioning his acquisition of Roman citizenship,
as found in fragment 4 (**lxxii) in *Sedis Incertae Fragmenta*?

2   Macrobius (*Sat.* 6.2.30), claims that Vergil based *Aen.* 9.672 ff. (Pan-
darus and Bitias throw open the gates of the Trojan camp) and *Aen.*
9.806 ff. (Turnus enters the camp) on two passages in Ennius, of which
only the second passage survives in this fragment. Skutsch, 558-559,
argues that the two Ennian passages stood in the same relation to
each other as the two Vergilian ones. A similar multiple allusion was
noted above, where Vergil describes the flames seen on Ascanius'
head and the confirmation of the omen (*Aen.* 2.679 ff.) by alluding
to *Annales* Book 3, where we find the portent of Tullius Servius and
the confirmation of the omen by thunderclap.

Book 16

Ennius returns in his old age to the composition of the *Annales* to add Books 16-18 (at the request of Nobilior?), possibly to defend the controversial actions of A. Manlius Vulso (brother of the consul Cn. Manlius Vulso and ally of Nobilior) during the Istrian War. See Skutsch, 569-570, for a discussion of E. Badian's suggestion that the exploits of the Caecilius brothers mentioned in fragment 6 (vi) may only be the ostensible reason for Ennius' resumption of the epic.

Ennius begins Book 16 with a proem.

1   Ennius alludes to his advanced age. Does the simile of the aged racehorse in fragment 2 (**lxix) of the *Sedis Incertae Fragmenta* belong here?

2   Another fragment from the proem which may describe the effect of old age.

3   *vetusta... bella* refers to wars already described in Books 1-15. *moveri = movere*.

4   Did Ennius contrast a king's proverbial quest for immortality with the ability of poets to bestow it? Horace, *Carm.* 3.30: *exegi monumentum...*, captures both ideas.
    ... quaerunt, aedificant nomen: Ennius transposes the direct objects of each verb.

5   A continuation of the idea that monuments are not everlasting.

6   The identity of these Caecilii Teucri is unknown.

Book 17

1   Macrobius claims that Vergil based *Aen.* 2.416-418 on this passage comparing the advancing of armies and storms, which is itself a combination of two Homeric similes (*Iliad* 9.4-8; 16.765-11). Skutsch, 594, points out that *Aen.* 10.355-361 also owes its inspiration to the Ennian passage.

Book 18

Did Ennius include a *sphragis*, perhaps the reference to his acquisition of Roman citizenship in *Sedis Incertae Fragmenta* 4 (**lxxii)? Like Naevius, Ennius announces the success of his poetry in an epitaph (in hexameter), which displays *carmen*-style verse effects:

> *aspicite, o cives, senis Enni imaginis formam.*
> *hic vestrum panxit maxima facta patrum.*

Nemo me dacrumis decoret, nec funera fletu
faxit. cur? Volito vivos per ora virum (Cic. *Tusc.* 1.34).

Sedis Incertae Fragmenta

1   Skutsch, 649, conjectures placing this fragment in Book 15, in the context of Fulvius Nobilior's founding of the Temple of the Muses.

2   The simile of the aged racehorse may belong in any number of places where Ennius could have alluded to his old age. Possible places suggested by Skutsch, 673, include the conclusion of Book 15, or Book 18, or even the proem of Book 16.

3   This reference to Ennius' age while composing the *Annales* is highly problematic. If Ennius began writing the epic around 184 BCE when he was 55 years old, the notice stating that he was 67 when he wrote Book 12 would mean he averaged one book a year. Skutsch, 675, however, argues that the dates mentioned by Varro are unlikely since it is probable that Ennius wrote Book 16, after an interval mentioned in that book, no later than 174 BCE when he was 65 years old.

4   Does Ennius allude to his acquisition of citizenship in the *Annales* to thank Nobilior for his patronage?

VI. COMEDY

Caecilius Statius

Plocium

1   The fiancé's father sings a polymetric canticum, filled with *carmen*-style verse effects, about his joyless marriage to his rich wife. Caecilius omits references to the wife's hideous appearance as found in Menander's text.
factis facit = figura etymologica.
salva urbe atque arce: inclusion of *arx* indicates a Roman reference not found in the Greek.
egomet inter vivos vivo mortuus: an effective joke for the contrast between life and death, but also for the proximity of the words *vivos vivo,* which belong to separate clauses, thus emphasizing his exclusion from the living.
plorando orando instando atque obiurgando: repetition of verbs with similar meanings renders his plight all the more ridiculous.

sermonem serit: this part of his speech describing his wife's vaunting among younger women is Caecilius' invention and adds much to the wife's caricature.

2   Rather than retain the generic description found in Menander of the shrewish character of the wife, Caecilius invents this passage, which illustrates the wife's shrewish antics.
ieiuna anima = bad breath.

4   Parmeno seems to realize that the girl is pregnant as he reckons the date of conception.

8   Musing on the tragedy of poverty. Caecilius adds the detail of the rich to Menander's text, thereby making the dire straits of the poor even more pronounced.
nam opulento famam // facile occultat factio: Caecilius draws attention to this line by using a *versus quadratus* with much alliteration.

13/14   The wedding is cancelled.

16/17   The bride's father intends to sue for the wedding expenses. Does the scene shift to a court scene?

18   It seems that the evidence proving the identity of the fiancé as the rapist has just been given, and the groom's family accepts responsibility.

19   Parmeno earns his freedom at the end of the play.

20   *catellae:* the context of this fragment is unknown.

VII. TRAGEDY II

Pacuvius

Antiopa

1   *...nati duo:* this fragment most likely comes from the prologue, since the true identity of the twins is known by the speaker.

2   The play apparently contained an extended philosophical debate between the twins about music, in which Zethus included a long digression on wisdom and the usefulness of virtue.

3   *loca horrida:* one of the twins charges the other with being uncouth and uncivilized, but as the next fragments reveal, the rivalry is really about sophistication and education.

4 The Chorus become contestants to Amphion's riddle and despite their name as *astici* they are not as sophisticated as the "rustic" twins. The erudite learning of the twins is reinforced by the obscure and novel vocabulary coined by Pacuvius.

tardigrada = a phrase coined by Pacuvius.

saeptuosa = obscure; a phrase coined by Pacuvius.

testudo = tortoise or lyre. Why does Pacuvius devote so many lines to a riddle which cannot advance the plot and simply gives a further example of the twins' rhetorical/sophistic education?

5 *inluvie* = *illuvies, ei*, feminine = filthy. As a pun on Antiopa's ugly appearance, Quintilian called the play "worty".

7 *fruges frendo sola saxi:* alliteration of f and s.

8 The context of this fragment is unclear but shows Pacuvius' interest in placing sophistic material within the play.

9 *minitabiliter* = threateningly; an adverb coined by Pacuvius.

14 *cor luctificabile* seems to be a direct quote from the play.

15 *inluvie*: repeated use of this word, which may have appeared throughout the play to reflect Antiopa's appearance and the degradation of her servitude to Dirce.

Teucer

1 The pile-up of adjectives is effective. The line begins with the alliteration of s and k/q sounds: *squale scabres,* and ends with the alliteration of t: *inculta vastitudine.*

2 *perrogitandod:* from *perrogito* (1) a verb only appearing in Pacuvius.

6 *Periere Danai, plera pars pessum datast:* heavy alliteration of p, d, and t.

9 *sapsa = ipsa.*

10 *accepso* = future of *accipio.*

12 A *canticum* in *octonarii* with heavy alliteration of s and t, which emphasize Telemon's anger; numerous elisions: *quom aetate exacta indigem.*

lacerasti orbasti exstinxti: three verbs, normally imperatives, are often found in succession in Roman tragedy, for an emphasis on pathos.

14 *retro citroque percito:* repetition and near rhyme to reflect the boat's rocking back and forth.

15 *strepitus fremitus clamor*: a pile-up of nouns, again for emphasis.

19 A formulaic line which resembles a *versus quadratus*.

Ex Incertis Fabulis

44 A famous passage often quoted to illustrate the inelegant nature of early Latin. However, the tortured description of dolphins may reflect Teucer's inability to describe creatures he had not seen before.

45 This passage, a vivid description of a storm at sea, is full of alliteration and assonance.

intuetur, nec tuendi: repetition of same verb.

tenebrae conduplicantur: the verb *conduplico* (to double) is used only here in Pacuvius, but also appears in Plautus and Terence. Of later writers, only Lucretius uses this verb in *DRN* 1.712 to add an archaic flavour to a passage about creation: *qui conduplicant primordia rerum aera iungentes igni terramque liquori.*

largifico = abundant; used only here and once by Lucretius: *DRN* 2.627.

50 *flexanima:* easily swayed or distracted. This verb appears twice in Pacuvius and only once afterwards in Catullus 64.330.

Accius

Medea sive Argonautae

The alternate titles reflect the large number of episodes and the competing themes in the play, revolving around Medea's assistance to Jason and the success of the Argonauts' mission.

1 The shepherd's inability to describe a ship is due to the fact that he has never seen one before; accordingly, his description is imprecise and based on the appearance and sound of the ship. The vocabulary mirrors the psychology of the shepherd.
Tanta moles: the description of the ship as a "heap" and the monster-like qualities would confuse the audience. This is a very effective opening since the shepherd rushes out, terrified, on stage. The scene piques the audience's curiosity, but it is not clear how this extended digression on the ignorance of the shepherd advances the plot.
prae se undas volvit, vortices vi suscitat;/ ruit prolapsa, pelagus respargit reflat: alliteration reinforces the idea of the ship lunging forward.
volvier = *volveri.*

Triton: mention of a seagod shows that the disturbance of the sea, at least in the mind of the shepherd, must have a supernatural cause. *Silvani:* Silvanus introduces a Roman element to the shepherd's description and reveals that he is not Asian.

2/3 The scene would be difficult to stage if we take the line literally.

6 *pavore pecuda... pascet postea:* heavy alliteration of p. The Shepherd's lament evokes bucolic poetry and may indicate Accius' mixing of literary genres.

8 *tristis turbinum toleraret:* alliteration of t.

9 *astu... lingua:* the emphasis on "city slickness" against one who is less clever is puzzling, since Apsyrtus is a prince.

lacto (1) = to entice.

10 *exul...expes expers:* the near rhyme of this alliteration is effective as Medea seeks sympathy for her plight.

12 In the 1968 reprint of Ribbeck's *RT,* Wolf-Hartmut Friedrich (xii-xiii), suggests that the line (based on Nonius) should read: *tun Diomedes es* and that the fragment belongs to Accius' *Diomedes.*

13 *...refelli...causandi locus:* legal terminology.

15 *lacrumis = lacrimis.*

16 *tabificabili:* an adjective created by Accius, appearing only here in all of extant Latin.

17 *Fors dominatur:* this sentiment seems generic for a play that contained much originality.

Ex Incertis Incertorum Fabulis

93 This passage is highly alliterative with p and t.

posquam = postquam.

Philocteta sive Philocteta Lemnius

The alternate titles reveal no essential difference, since Philoctetes is the play's protagonist and events unfold on the island of Lemnos.

1 An extremely elevated address with heavy alliteration of p and c. The lines have a certain *versus quadratus* quality to them, with most periods occuring at the end of the line.

2 *praesto:* the Chorus point out those local landmarks with mythological significance.

occulta coluntur: near rhyme.

Volcania: Vulcan was thrown from heaven by Jupiter for defending his mother. He landed on Lemnos but was afterwards lame from the fall. Philoctetes also suffers from a foot injury, and it is significant that Vulcan is connected to the play's action.

ignis...mortalibus clam divusus: a reference to Prometheus' gift of fire to humankind.

3   *habet* here means to live.

4   *caprigenum trita ungulis*: as with his appearance, Philoctetes' remote location indicates that he has assumed the habits of a savage beast.

5   *pro veste pinnis ... textis*: Philoctetes' appearance underscores how removed he is from civilization.

6   *est eundum... captandum mihi*: it is rare to find a double future passive periphrastic in Roman tragedy.

9   *tela*: this is the first extant reference in the play to Philoctetes' bow, which is the reason for Odysseus' embassy.

11   The alliteration of v, t, and c reflect Philoctetes' pain and anger.

13   *tesqua loca*: a term of unknown meaning from augury, which seems here to refer to a wild location.

14   *aspernabilis*: an adjective first coined by Accius and not used again until Aulus Gellius in the second century CE.

taetritudo: an expression coined and only used by Accius.

faxsit = faciet.

15   *novem hiemes*: this chronological reference reminds the audience how long Philoctetes has been suffering apart from the Greeks and how long it has taken them to visit him. This is more an indictment against the Greeks than it is a comment on how long the war has lasted up to this point, since Odysseus must address this lapse of time if he is to retrieve the bow from Philoctetes.

16   *Arm' erg'ignav'invict'es fabricatus manu*: this line contains four elisions and reflects Philoctetes' agitated state.

17   To underscore the softness of the Phrygians, Philoctetes employs alliteration of m and two elisions.

18   *Pari dyspari, si inpar*: pun on the name Paris?

19   *vis vulneris ulceris*: alliteration which approaches rhyme.

VIII. SATIRE

Lucilius

Satires

The original title of Lucilius' satires does not survive – *Carmina*? *Sermones*? Since Books 26-30 were written first, Book 1 is actually Book 6; Lucilius may have adapted the original contents of Book 6 to serve as the first book of the revised collection.

Book 1

1 *consilium*: parody of epic, including Ennius' *Annales*.

   summis ... de rebus: ironic since the gods normally trouble themselves little over humans. Seneca's satiric *Apocolocyntosis* contains a council of the gods who ridicule mankind, and the dead emperor Claudius in particular.

2 *servare* = to save Rome from moral decay.

3 *pater*: humour is achieved by Apollo calling all of the mentioned gods "father." A satiric comment on the large number of gods in the Roman pantheon?

4 The council of the gods included an attack against Cornelius Lentulus Lupus (died 123 BCE).

Book 2

From a council of the gods, the narrative shifts to the present. Rather than an epic battle, as one might expect from the epic framework or epic invocation at the beginning of the *Satires,* Lucilius recounts events (and speeches?) surrounding a famous trial.

Book 3

Lucilius' description of a journey to Sicily is the model for Horace's "Journey to Brindisium" (*Serm.* 1.5). If Horace's satire is any indication, Lucilius mocked the speech and customs of provincial Italians he encountered along the way.

1 *labosum* = slippery; this is the only extant use of the word.

2 *susque...deque*: adverb: both up and down, therefore of no consequence.
   montes: an exaggeration, since the hills which Lucilius mentions are small.

3   *nox* = *nocte* (according to Servius, *ad Aen.* 10.244).

4   *Caupona...Syra:* just one of the colorful people encountered by Lucilius.

Book 4

Lucilius' description of a gladiatorial combat takes on a mock epic tone as he presents a contest between two fighters, Aeserninus and Pacideianus, and one's taunting of the other, which may have been answered in a speech by Aeserninus.

1   *Flaccorum munere*: the *ludi* (funeral?) were sponsored by the Flaccus family.
spurcus = filthy.
loco = station in life.
conponitur = was matched against...

2   *Occidam...vincam*: repetition of idea, since one wins if one kills one's opponent.
iratus: unlike the ideal of an epic hero, Pacideianus makes his hostility towards his opponent clear and derives strength from it.

Book 5

The custom of visiting a sick friend (*amicus*) was not just a friendly gesture, it was a social obligation practised by the upper classes.

1   *tam etsi non quaeris*: this seems to be an even bigger cause for complaint.
Eissocratium = Isocrates; is the Latinized spelling of his name an example of Lucilius' interest in lexography?
lerodesque: the Greek word for trash.
miraciodes = altogether childish.

Book 6

Lucilius presents an encounter between a historical personality (the influential aristocrat Scipio Aemilianus) and an unnamed bore. While the encounter may be entirely fictional, we cannot rule out that some such episode was reported to Lucilius by Aemilianus. This book was the model for Catullus 23 and 24 and Horace *Serm.* 1.9

1   *bulga*: knapsack or wallet. The repetition of this word reinforces the idea of the man's vulgarity, in particular the phrase *cum bulga cenat, dormit, lavit.*

Book 7

The dramatic context of this Book does not survive, but the episode quoted here describes a jilted lover and his planned self-mutilation for revenge. This scene, and possibly other episodes from Book 7, seems to have been a model for Petronius' *Satyricon*, in particular the argument between Encolpius and Ascyltus over Giton.

1   *testa,ae* = sherd, which emphasizes the violence and may be a pun on *testis*.

Book 8

This book also contains sexual material but the fragments are too few to reconstruct descriptions with any certainty.

Book 9

1   *poema*: the splitting of hairs over the meaning of the words poem and poetry (*poesis*) may be an example of the sort of literary argument Lucilius had with Accius.

Book 10

A literary dispute between Lucilius and Accius?

Books 11-14

Book 11 contains character sketches of prominent Romans, but the fragments from Books 12-14 are too few to determine the themes of the satires they contained. Juvenal in his *Satires* purposely selects dead Romans as safe targets, so perhaps it is Lucilius' aristocratic position which allows him to write about members of his own class.

Book 15

Book 15, which considered philosophical and religious questions, may have influenced Lucretius.

1   *Polyphemus*: the cyclops encountered by Odysseus in the *Odyssey*.
malus = mast.
corbita = cargo.

2   *Terriculas* = creatures.
Lamia = witch.
Fauni...Pompilii...Numae: Pompilius Numa, as mentioned in Ennius' *Annales*, was considered a reformer of religion. His mention here with Fauns points to the superstituous nature of beliefs associated with him.

omnia ficta: the simile of children fearing statues is poignant and effective for Lucilius' argument that one should not fear ghosts and goblins.

Book 16

Porphyrio's notice that Horace's character Lalage is derived from Lucilius' Collyra indicates that Book 16 was elegiac in nature.

Books 17-19

The context of these books is unclear from the few surviving fragments.

Book 20

A book devoted to a *cena* that may have served as one of the literary models for Petronius' *Cena Trimalchionis.*

Book 21

No fragments survive.

Books 22-25

In these books Lucilius seems to describe his freedmen and slaves in elegiac couplets.

Book 26

Formerly Book 1 of the unrevised collection, written in Saturnians.

1. *Persium non curo legere, Laelium Decumum volo:* Lucilius here imitates Callimachus, who advertised his literary taste for concise, elegant poems in his poetry. Gaius Persius was a very learned grammarian and scholar. Catullus adopts a similar tone in the first poem of his collection, in which he mocks the learnedness of Cornelius Nepos.

2. *hic cruciatur....:* a reference to an author punished for outspokenness, in the model of Naevius?

4. *Popili* = Popilius Laenas, who was defeated by the Numantines in 138 BCE.
   ...cane: the interlocutor urges Lucilius to write panegyrics for the rich and famous as Ennius did in order to secure the patronage of M. Fulvius Nobilior.

5. *folliculo* = bag; bladder. Lucilius' attack against the interlocutor is extremely vulgar and recalls Catullus' invectives.
   editus = dropped (as in excrement).

Book 27

Dedication of Book 27 to Scipio Aemilianus?

   1.   *Popli*: Scipio Aemilianus?
       studiose = learned in an Hellenistic sense.
       sedulo = earnest.

Book 28

Book 28 seems to contain three satires in various meters, but the contexts of only two are recoverable: a philosophical discourse set in Athens, and the circumstances surrounding the attack and lawsuit of a Roman citizen.

Book 29

Book 29 contains five satires in various meters. Themes include behavior towards women (in sexual contexts), criticism of tragedy and comedy, and the activities of men in Rome.

   1.   This fragment comes from the second satire in this book in which Lucilius describes a *cena*.

   2.   Possibly from the fourth satire in Book 29, this fragment criticizes the convoluted *exordia* from Pacuvius' tragedies.

Book 30

The three fragments cited under Book 30 come from the second satire in which Lucilius has a literary dispute with a comic writer.

   1.   *haurire*: Lucilius seems to borrow this desciption, of a poet drinking from the fountain of the Muses, from Ennius (based on Lucretius *DRN* 1.926f: *avia Pieridum peragro loca...iuvat integros accedere fontes atque haurire*).

   2.   *Camenae*: "to me a mortal, the *Camenae* entrust their bolts." Lucilius refers to both the Greek Muses and the Italic *Camenae* in this satire, however, the extant fragments do not allow readers to draw distinctions between the two.

   3.   male dicere = to slander.